ULTIMATE KEMPO

ULTIMATE
KEMPO

THE SPIRIT AND TECHNIQUE
OF KOSHO RYU

*A Study in Movement, Motion and
Balance for Effective Self-defense*

by JEFF DRISCOLL

With a foreword by
BRUCE JUCHNIK

TUTTLE PUBLISHING
Tokyo • Rutland, Vermont • Singapore

Published by Tuttle Publishing, an imprint of Periplus Editions (HK) Ltd., with editorial offices at 364 Innovation Drive, North Clarendon, Vermont 05759 U.S.A. and at 61 Tai Seng Avenue #02-12, Singapore 534167.

Instructional photos by Linda Mullins
Japan photos by Jeff Driscoll
Shaka in photos by Alexzander Warasta
Mizu no kokoru kanji by Cindy Jutras.
Budo kanji by Michael Brown

Library of Congress Cataloging-in-Publication Data
Driscoll, Jeff.
  Ultimate kempo: the spirit and technique of kosho ryu / Jeff Driscoll.
      p. cm.
  ISBN 978-0-8048-4123-8 (pbk.)
1. Kung fu. I. Title.
  GV1114.7.D75 2010
  796.815'9--dc22

                                      2009030881

ISBN 978-0-8048-4123-8

Distributed by

North America, Latin America & Europe
Tuttle Publishing
364 Innovation Drive
North Clarendon, VT 05759-9436 U.S.A.
Tel: 1 (802) 773-8930; Fax: 1 (802) 773-6993
info@tuttlepublishing.com
www.tuttlepublishing.com

Asia Pacific
Berkeley Books Pte. Ltd.
61 Tai Seng Avenue #02-12
Singapore 534167
Tel: (65) 6280-1330; Fax: (65) 6280-6290
inquiries@periplus.com.sg
www.periplus.com

Japan
Tuttle Publishing
Yaekari Building, 3rd Floor
5-4-12 Osaki
Shinagawa-ku
Tokyo 141 0032
Tel: (81) 3 5437-0171; Fax: (81) 3 5437-0755
tuttle-sales@gol.com

14 13 12 11 10   10 9 8 7 6 5 4 3 2 1

Printed in Singapore

Contents

Dedication

This book is dedicated to two very special teachers, Thomas and Barbara Driscoll. I am very thankful to have two of the most wonderful parents any son could hope for. They taught me many things throughout the years.

They taught me to be kind and compassionate towards other people. They taught me that hard work and having goals and dreams defines a successful person. But most of all, they taught me to have respect for all that I come in contact with. Respect seems to have become a forgotten quality these days. For all that you've done, and all the incredibly important lessons you've taught me, I thank you. I love you, Mom and Dad.

**This book is also dedicated to the memory of
Thomas Mayer 1939-2007**

Every once in a while, someone comes into your life for only a short time, but leaves a dramatic impact. Thomas was that type of person. He was one of the most courageous, intelligent, and insightful people, that I have had the pleasure to meet and spend time with.

I miss you, Thomas.

Jeff Driscoll

Foreword

I am very honored to be writing the foreword to this text. The reader of this book will gain a better understanding and insight into its author and his experiences in the arts. Jeff is the eternal student. He makes great sacrifice in his journey to attain knowledge and understanding of these arts. Pay special attention to his writing on "Budo."

There are many misconceptions in the arts regarding "Budo" and what it truly is. By reading this text you will understand its true meaning. "Budo" is not represented just in the actions of a man; it is his spirit.

Based on his experience and study of a variety of arts, Driscoll Sensei has reached a high level of accomplishment in many ways. You will see which arts he has gravitated to and you will understand why. He chose to explore arts that matched his spirit, strength, and passion and those that were well suited to him as a practitioner that is why he has been so successful. Not all arts are right for everyone. Driscoll Sensei has chosen well and knows the way of the warrior.

Bruce Juchnik, Hanshi

CHAPTER 1

What is Kosho Shorei Ryu Kempo?

Philosophy

Kosho literally means "old pine tree." Shorei translates as "school of encouragement." A traditional ryu is a school of thought pertaining to an art form. The origins of Kosho Shorei Ryu as we know it today stems from the meditations of a Japanese Buddhist priest named Kosho Bosatsu. This name, literally translated, means "Old Pine Tree Buddha." This is a general name that sheds little light on the true identity of the man. But the name is less important than the result of his meditations.

Around the year 1235 AD, this priest meditated under an old pine tree. As a priest, his Buddhist studies taught him pacifism, which were an apparent contradiction to the destructive arts in which he was also trained. It was this contradiction that caused him to seek a place where he could meditate. As many monks before him, he chose the old pine tree where, it was believed, the spirit of the Buddha had fled.

Entrance to Temple Grounds

Temple Grounds Sign

View of some of the 3333 steps　　　　　　**Temple Gateway**

It was during this period of meditation that he was enlightened. The revelation led to his discovery of universal laws and natural principles pertaining to our existence and the resolution of conflict. The Sei Kosho Shorei Kai International encourages students to move toward this same enlightenment through studying natural law.

Kempo means "Fist Law." This is the Kosho Shorei Ryu form of martial arts; but it is much more than the law of the fist. The predecessors of Kempo are Chuan Fa, in China, and before that Vajra Mukti in India. Kempo's philosophy is to study and understand man's relationship with nature.

Kempo is the study of natural law pertaining to mankind. Kempo does not just deal with the physical arts; it also deals with the spiritual side of oneself, and mankind's understanding of itself.

Gateway Close Up　　　　　　**Entrance to Main Temple Building**

Traditionally, Kempo students have studied much more than the physical martial arts. They also study philosophical classics, including the *I Ching*: *the Book of Changes*. They study the five elements and the *In* and *Yo* (Yin and Yang in Chinese). They understand the principle of balance, and how one can, through understanding balance, exist harmoniously with the whole of mankind. Within their own realm, in their own reality, they learn how to adjust their reality, behavior, or physical presence within others' perception of reality. Primarily, they study themselves: Body, mind, and spirit. This microcosm leads to the understanding of all things.

Kempo, therefore means study, and practice, and the discipline of study and practice. The understanding of this philosophy, the embodiment of this practice, and the reality of this study prepares the Kempo-ka for possible conflict. In this study, defending one's self becomes very easy.

Kosho is a way of life and an understanding of the process of life. Understanding the process of a fight is the key. Techniques used in a fight are only a small part of that process. What happens before that point is of primary importance.

Kosho Ryu warrior-monks and other practitioners have used the study, and the practical application of this study, successfully throughout history. In the late 1500's, 5,000 samurai attacked Shaka-In, the temple grounds on which the now-famous old pine tree still stands. Using Kosho Shorei Ryu Kempo, the 400 monks living and training there engaged in combat against the onslaught, successfully protecting some of the most important artifacts and property of the temple grounds, including the famous old pine tree itself.

The martial prowess of the Kosho Shorei monks was well known among the Japanese at the time, and was feared by many Daimyo as well as their swordsmen. It was the practice of this philosophy of study that gave the monks their edge. This philosophy was adopted by many of Japan's greatest and most famous swordsmen, including Musashi Miyamoto.

The success of Kosho Ryu today is apparent in the large numbers of students and teachers gravitating to these studies. Many teachers with decades of experience are reexamining their training based on the uniqueness and startling pertinence of what they see in a Kosho Ryu seminar.

Many of these teachers and students have said that the combat-effectiveness of Kosho is simply at a higher level than anything they had seen previously. Yet, Kosho Ryu concepts had often never even been considered in their previous training.

Kosho Ryu was brought to Hawaii and therefore to the United States in the 1940's by James Mitose.

The philosophical teachings, which were largely ignored by many of Mitose Sensei's early students, (with the notable exception of the late Thomas Young) play a major role in the manifestation of the physical combative arts of Kosho Ryu. Without them, true understanding of Kempo is not possible. Kempo is not a martial art—It is much more.

James Mitose (center) and his 6 Black Belts.

Look for Similarities

The Kosho Ryu practitioner studies natural law. In so doing, he has the ability to see similarities in all movement. Therefore he holds no prejudice toward or against other styles or martial systems. Kosho Ryu practitioners understand that the only real differences between martial arts pertain

Temple Grounds Map

to the cultures from which they come. Cultures produce various tendencies that shape the way arts are taught. Although teaching methods are delivery modes for the understanding of the essence of an art, the arts themselves are very similar. Bruce Juchnik Hanshi is well qualified to make a statement such as this. He holds mastery-level knowledge and certification in over ten distinct martial art forms.

Kosho Shorei Ryu Kempo originated in Japan. To practitioners, Kosho Ryu's Chinese roots are apparent in its basic philosophy. Because Kosho teaches them to look for similarities, they see no substantial difference between Kosho and studies from Korea, Indonesia, China, or America.

All human beings move basically the same way. All motion is related. The same emotions are experienced by all of mankind. Fundamentally, human beings are similar, throughout continents, cultures, and time.

Natural Law

The study of physics is only part of the understanding of Natural Law. Kosho Ryu Kempo-ka also studies the natural laws of our basic individual philosophy. One can understand the physics of both our internal and external structures. Students seek to understand who they are as they relate to others based upon their past experiences and prejudices.

Body movement changes, much like personalities change, based on an individual's momentary and long-term mind-sets and their physical prejudices. Understanding that both they themselves and potential adversaries are governed by these natural laws. Kempo-ka apply a great many strategies to handle potential conflicts successfully. This is what makes it possible to defeat an opponent without throwing a blow. In fact, it is possible to defeat an opponent by strategically manipulating his ki (mind set in this case). These are based on an understanding of his prejudices, in such a way as to make him decide to never attack you in the first place! Psychology is physics applied to the mind.

Objective

The objective of the Kosho Ryu Kempo-ka is to be able to relate to everything, abandon prejudices, and thus rid conflict from life. Conflict is usually created from differences of opinion pertaining to physical or philosophical prejudices. Once you eliminate conflict (emotional or physical) and understand laws and principles, you learn to see yourself as the root of all of your conflict.

Once the source of conflict is known, it can be eliminated. Happiness is the result. Kempo-ka become content, able to harmo-

The View From the Summit

nize with and accept life's events, and able to control their environment. Once you learn to control yourself and your environment, controlling or redirecting an attacker is possible as well.

Kempo

While Kempo literally translates from Japanese as "Fist Law," its meaning can be traced back to what is called the mudra, which are hand postures. Each of kempo's hand postures represent both the physical and the spiritual realm. These realms are inexorably linked. Kempo itself is an entity. It is not a style of martial arts or a form of techniques.

Yet this is a difficult concept to understand and therefore in our society today it is, unfortunately, largely looked upon as a martial art.

James Mitose Sensei, explained that Kempo is a philosophy. Mitose brought Kosho Shorei Ryu Kempo from Japan to the United States as a philosophy of growth, of study, and of struggle. The martial arts become simple, even self-evident, through understanding the process of these three elements.

Within Kosho Ryu Kempo, there are many sub-arts of study. The purpose of the study of various different art forms is to learn to see the similarities in all of them. Three general categories of study are the healing arts, the cultural arts, and the martial arts. All three are interwoven.

The study of healing arts helps the martial artist understand anatomical strengths and weaknesses as well as the natural flow of energy and how that energy might be directed. In turn the martial arts help the healer better understand the practical application through the study of movement.

The cultural arts play a similar role. Included in the cultural arts is the study of history or densho, an important element in both the martial and healing arts. Language is also studied from all perspectives. The study of the Japanese language creates the ability in the disciplined student of Kosho Ryu to understand the history and cultures of other people. This in turn ties in with the philosophy of looking for similarities, eliminating prejudice and conflict, and creating happiness and peace in their lives.

Each of the many sub-arts of study in Kosho Ryu eventually intertwines. Aruki waza, for instance, which is a combative technique involving proper posturing toward an opponent in Bujutsu, is also utilized in the studies of swordsmanship, shodo (ancient Japanese brush calligraphy), and healing arts. This type of lesson initially brings students to confusion. Eventually, it allows them to understand Mu, nothingness. That is the purpose of the study of Kempo in Kosho Shorei Ryu. Once that is accomplished, one sees everything, and at the same time realizes that it is really nothing.

Hanshi Bruce Juchnik and the Sei Kosho Shorei Kai supplied this information.

CHAPTER 2

The Objective

Mind Like Water

As we go through life on our journey as martial artists, we learn many lessons – some martial lessons, some life lessons. If we look deeper into these lessons, we start to see that the two are connected. Principles we learn while studying martial arts start to have a direct relation to much needed principles/concepts that help guide us on our journey in life. This also works the other way around.

Let's take a look at the concept of Mizu No Kokoro or "Mind Like Water," which involves having a mind that is not "stuck," but flowing and constantly changing to adapt to circumstances we encounter. This concept is extremely important to leading a fulfilling life. As individuals, we all have problems, challenges, and hardships that come our way. If we focus only on the problems, challenges and hardships, instead of the solutions or actions, our mind becomes

"stuck." Having this frame of mind is not conducive to solving problems or finding a course of action that will allow us to overcome these obstacles.

After all, the willingness to take action to deal with these challenges in life is what makes us stronger, well-adjusted individuals on this journey. If we focus on the solution instead of the problem, our mind takes on the mannerisms of water, which finds its way around, over, under, or through whatever obstacle in its path.

If we train our minds to take on this attitude when it comes to our martial arts, we are free

to flow with whatever comes our way, making adjustments in order to accomplish our goal–the defeat of our opponents. So, how do we arrive at this place of freedom?

In my mind, it all comes down to study. We must study movement, motion, manipulation of balance, and structure. We must break free of being bound by the technique we are trying to apply and see what concepts govern the specific situation. By gaining an understanding of the principles and concepts that make a martial technique work, we build ourselves an arsenal of options. Having options allows us to flow with whatever comes our way and gives us the tools needed to accomplish our goal.

This book is intended to open the reader's eyes in several ways. In the martial sense, the objective is to provide the reader with the tools to look deeper into his or her art, to see concepts and principles that apply to all martial arts styles and systems. This process leads to a better understanding of the art we practice and at the same time, opens our eyes to the incredible amount of options available to us.

On the other hand, this book is meant to expose readers to (or remind them of) concepts which lead to a more fulfilling life and to offer principles by which to help them become more confident, compassionate, and understanding individuals.

One very important point: we cannot underestimate the importance of learning the basics. A student cannot just "jump ahead" to the more advanced, intricate techniques and concepts. We must all go through a progression of training (Shugyo no Junjo). This process starts with the individual making up his/her mind to dedicate the time and effort necessary, making it a priority in life. The student must also make up his/her mind to learn well the basics of the art, the fundamentals that lay the solid groundwork of a good martial artist. We must then sharpen and develop ourselves through countless repetition, eventually evolving into a master who has not only developed the physical attributes necessary to the art, but also the mental and internal attributes.

Qualities such as respect, compassion, patience and perseverance, and the freedom to not be governed by circumstances, are a by-product of martial arts training.

In this process, we undergo a transformation similar to that of the forging of a Japanese katana. During this process, we must push ourselves through countless hours of training and repetition, constant corrections by our teachers, pushing ourselves physically and mentally until we are honed and sharpened into an instrument that has the strength to handle any challenge, and the compassion and understanding to contribute to a better society.

In the following chapters, you will find various techniques and examples, which are used as a vehicle to apply these concepts or principles. Understand that these techniques are just my way of conveying the message...there are countless other techniques and variations which may apply also.

This book is about simply opening doors for the practitioner, so he or she may grasp the concept, and in turn experiment and discover how to apply it for themselves. It is my belief, that the art should fit the person...not the person should have to fit the art. The beauty of Kosho Ryu Kempo is that the understanding of concepts/principles, allows for many options and avenues, so the art may fit the practitioner.

CHAPTER 3

What is the Martial Way ?
Why Study It ?

The Way of the Warrior

In my limited 28 years of martial arts experience, I won't even begin to claim that I understand the concept of Budo. How Budo is explained and defined differs from person to person. The best I can do is relate to what my teachers have tried to instill in me, and what the concept of Budo has come to mean to me.

Budo translates to 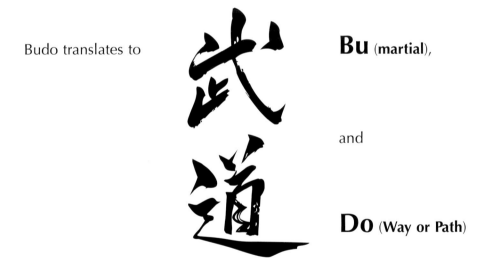 **Bu** (martial),

and

Do (Way or Path)

To me, Budo is using the martial arts as a vehicle to train the mind and the body. It's about character building and forging the spirit through the challenges put before us in our martial arts training, much like that of the forging of the Japanese katana—building strength layer after layer. It's about giving just a little more, when our mind and body is telling us there is no more.

It's about training and mastering your mind so that you are no longer governed by or reacting to environmental influences or circumstances, yet always being aware of them and allowing you to see things for what they really are.

Budo is about having the attitude of a warrior and living with a sense of honor in everything that you do.

It's about being strong yet compassionate for everyone, working for the betterment of yourself and of the community you live in. These are not easy things to work towards, much less accomplish! Lord knows we're not perfect.

But it's about the path. It's about the challenges that are put before us and how we respond to them. It's about the development of a moral code we build for ourselves, with the help and guidance of our teachers.

It's all about the process!

The Battle of Life

Even though most of us never step out onto the battlefield with sword in hand to face an opponent whose objective is to physically destroy us, we still face many battles and conflicts everyday. Having the attitude of a compassionate warrior is an extremely useful tool on our journey through life. We must also recognize that our most difficult opponent is one we deal with everyday...ourselves.

What are some of the battles we face as martial artists and human beings? Sometimes it's the simple yet difficult battle of getting out of bed when the alarm goes off. It is certainly easier to just hit the snooze button. Maybe it's the battle of motivating ourselves to have a positive attitude for our work, or towards the people we come in contact with each day. Maybe, it's the battle of being better focused in our martial arts training, or digging a little deeper physically when your body and mind is telling you to stop. If we don't give that little extra push, how will we know what we can truly become?

It's Really Up to You.

We all have related battles to face in life. We all have challenges that we face everyday—deadlines, accomplishment of goals, stress, and environmental factors. Budo teaches us when we have battles/challenges. We must focus our energies on the solution, not the problem.

It's what you do with what is laid before you that really matters! Is the cup either half-full or half empty? It's all about how you perceive things. There is always a battle, a situation in which we are tested, in everyone's life, no matter what your occupation, financial situation or family background.

Pain is part of life...misery is optional!

I believe that challenges come our way for a reason. Sometimes it's hard to see the positive in situations, but there is usually a lesson to learn or a reason we are being tested. How we deal with them is up to us. We can allow these challenges/battles to steal from us our strength and our vision of who we want to be. Or we can use them to forge our spirit, making us more confident, disciplined, and happy people. As we become better people, we start to affect our communities by having a positive impact on society. As a teacher, my job is to act as a guide for people looking to embark on this journey, helping them become capable leaders and contribute to society.

Can you start a human revolution?
What kind of difference can you make?

Life as a Warrior

An individual who lives with the attitude of a warrior takes on a different view of the world. Budo is the philosophy that guides a warrior and shapes the way he or she sees these events or challenges.

Do we look at things from all perspectives?
Do we try to recognize and understand other people's motivations for what they do? More
   importantly, do we realize our own motivations for our actions?
Are our own motivations pure in the sense that we strive for the benefit of ourselves, as
   well as for the benefit of all parties involved? Or are we motivated strictly by our own
   selfish desires?

Everything we do, in every personal relationship, business relationship, transaction or deal we make, there must be a mutual benefit for all. This is not a principle that most people live by in today's society! Having a sense of honor in what we do, and how we treat people, is needed now more than ever. Developing the ability to understand other people's motivations by observing their actions is an extremely important skill. Someone whose motivation was not that obvious has fooled us all. We end up disappointed, hurt emotionally and sometimes financially. Considering one's motivation before taking action can sometimes save us from this disappointment.

Honor

Do you have a code of honor?
Do you have a sense of what is right and wrong?
Do you have the courage to stand up for what you believe is right, even when it is
   unpopular?

I believe true Budo teaches this. Sometimes we need to be a voice for what is right, even though it may jeopardize our position or others' view of us. This can be a tough situation to be in, but if we have a code of honor, and conviction for the betterment of something, we must take a stand.

Taking this position can be scary and unpopular. But usually, if our intentions are pure, good will come of it. Sometimes, taking an unpopular stand is much better than living with the regret of doing nothing.

When we speak of honor, we have to think in terms of right and wrong.

Where's the line?
How far can you go before you cross that line?
Does a line even exist?

Realize that sometimes in life, environmental influences exist that compels us to make compromises that we would not normally make. Compromise is important, but not at the expense of our honor. Remember that once you step over the line of right and wrong too many times, that line begins to disappear. We must do our best to keep our honor and ourselves in check.

The Constant of Change

Do you recognize the fragility of life?
Do you know what tomorrow holds?
Do you recognize that in a blink of an eye many of the things that we are blessed with can be taken away?
If you were to find out that you had only six months left on this earth, what would you do differently?
Would you be a better husband, father, teacher, or person in general?
Would you treat people in a kinder, more compassionate manner?
Would you really listen to the people who are close to you, and try to better understand what is important to them?
Would you learn or attempt something you've always wanted to do, but were afraid to?

Would you contribute something that would make a profound difference in the lives of other people, therefore leaving a piece of yourself behind...your legacy perhaps?

What will your legacy be?
What will people say when you're gone?
Will it be positive?
Will people remember sacrifices and contributions you've made, whether they were contributions of time, money, or just of yourself?

Oh! That's right, you will probably be here in six months. But with this philosophy and discipline, we can change our future actions and our appreciation of things in our life. Living with the philosophy of Budo in our lives gives us an appreciation for these blessings and allows us to see that nothing is permanent and things will always continue to change.

Respect

Do you understand the concept of respect, and that we must strive to respect others even if we don't understand them? The martial way is all about respect! We must learn to respect our elders for the work they have done and the dues they have paid. Their experience in life can give us much insight and if we're lucky enough, maybe they'll share some of their knowledge and insights to make our journey a little smoother.

Conflict

So, if we are looking for an avenue of self-improvement, why train in the martial arts? What does martial arts training give us that is difficult to find elsewhere? Martial arts training teaches us about conflict and how to find better ways to deal with it. In it's most basic interpretation, training in the martial arts teaches an individual how to deal with the conflict of an aggressive, attacking individual. The goal is to first build physical skills and abilities to neutralize the threat of physical violence. Building the qualities of speed, power, balance and stability, along with eye training in the context of the art's basic fundamentals is essential in this stage.

In the more advanced aspects of this stage, students learn how to be more subtle and refined with their techniques and strategies. They will learn how to properly use angles to evade their attacker, enabling them to use their techniques more efficiently, as well as taking advantage of using the attacker's force against them. At this stage, students should also learn strategies to enable them to manipulate the structure and balance of an attacker. Someone who cannot find balance cannot follow through with a powerful, effective attack.

As students progress through this first stage and learn how to deal with the physical conflict of an attacker, they should start to see the connection between dealing with the physical attack of an opponent and the non-physical arena of conflict in everyday life. This realization seldom occurs without a teacher who can expose students to the proper philosophies of the martial arts, and can point out the similarities of these conflicts. It is said that a good teacher can take you places that you've never been, while a great teacher can dramatically change the place you're in. So, it is extremely important to have a teacher who can point out the necessary keys to enlighten the student to the fact that these comparisons exist. However, a true student of the arts may turn to many different sources for instruction, including any resource of written or verbal information that enhances the student's perspective of these comparisons.

When we talk about conflict in a nonphysical sense, we have to think about the conflict that exists in our personal relationships, business/professional relationships, financial situations, and any type of situation in our life where we feel a sense of conflict. Strategies of warfare directly relate to daily life conflict. In warfare it is extremely important to know or understand our enemy.

Is it any less important to understand our spouse, co-workers, or family? In order to avoid or overcome conflict with people with whom we have relationships or dealings, we must not only understand them but also what's important to them. Seeing their perspective on things goes a long way when it comes to avoiding conflict or overcoming it. That is not to say what we must agree with it, but being able to acknowledge their point of view is critical in resolving conflict. Sometimes, we must agree to disagree on issues!

Ever wonder why groups of people cannot get along with one another, even when they share the same perspectives and beliefs? Why is there always some sort of conflict? A certain amount of conflict will always exist among groups of people simply because every individual has a certain amount of internal conflict. Budo and the martial arts teaches us to recognize these inner conflicts, and gives us the strength to work towards eliminating them.

This is NOT an easy task.

It may certainly take a lifetime! Not only is it beneficial to work at eliminating these conflicts for the purpose of leading a more balanced life, but also it is essential in helping us make good decisions in a world of many choices. Nowadays, life is extremely fast-paced, and we are constantly bombarded with choices. I believe that working towards eliminating or gaining control over these inner conflicts produces a clearer, more receptive mind, and hones our instincts—all of which helps us to make better decisions and choices.

It all comes down to balance—external and internal. Ever notice how internal conflicts come to the surface, when we are feeling pressured by environmental influences? These pressures can come from many different environmental influences, such as money or financial matters, personal relationships, professional pressures and deadlines, health issues or any number of things life may bring our way. Conflicts and insecurities, which exist inside us, will come to the surface when pressured by these influences, squeezed from us like squeezing a grape produces grape juice. What lies inside us, is what comes out under pressure. While writing this book, I had the pleasure of being in Japan with several of my teachers. During this time a terrible earthquake struck the countries of Pakistan and India. It was amazing to me, as I watched CNN, (one of only two channels in English), how two countries which disliked each other immensely, were working together for a common good.

Why must it sometimes take a catastrophe or some tragic event to bring out the good in human nature?

Why can we not have a compassionate and helpful attitude towards the people and situations we come in contact with everyday?

Is it because we are very often totally absorbed in our own selfish wants and needs?

Is it because we all have a certain amount of conflict inside ourselves?

Do we even recognize how this inner conflict affects our perspective of things and people around us?

The Progression of Training

Shugyo no Junyo is a concept used in the martial arts that pertains to the actual progression of training. The formula for this progression of training is very simple:

1) Make up your mind to learn the basic fundamentals of your chosen art. This means setting aside the time and energy required to practice and learn the fundamentals.

2) Repetition and constant practice of the techniques and lessons pertaining to your art.

3) Eventually, evolving into a person who has mastered the art and is confident and in control of his/her environment.

Pretty simple formula...though not necessarily easy to do! Now, if we look at this formula for training, should we not also see that this is also a formula for life?

We, as practitioners of the martial arts, must look towards the lessons contained in our studies. Look at the principle of avoidance, and how we use this on an attacker who is trying to harm us. First, we need to keep our vision peripheral so we may see all of what is going on around us. If we see the situation far in advance, it becomes very easy to avoid it. Secondly, we must move at the right time. Not necessarily fast, but on time. Timing is everything!

When dealing with a non-physical confrontation with a friend, acquaintance, or spouse, the same basic considerations must come into play. We must strive to see situations before they become confrontations. If the conflict is not something we desire or need to be involved in, why allow ourselves to be drawn into it? When someone wishes to engage in an argument or debate with you, and you can see that this particular person only sees things from their own perspective, refuse to allow yourself to be involved. One of my teacher's favorite quotes is, "Never argue with a fool, for he may be doing the same." It's very difficult to argue or debate with someone who refuses to engage. This is a simple example of the principle of avoidance.

Redirection is also a concept to be used in a verbal conflict. If we are to redirect someone's direction or force, we must strive to make them focus on something other than their primary objective. In a physical arena, this could be a painful strike used to put the opponent mentally and physically off-balance. In the verbal arena, this could be merely redirecting the conversation, maybe getting the person to talk about himself or something important to him. Who doesn't want to talk about themselves or something of interest?

As martial artists, we need to pay attention to the principles of avoidance, redirection, and creating imbalance that we use when dealing with physical conflict, and apply them in the arenas of personal and business relationships, as well as all of our social interactions.

Life's Cycle of Progression

How do we start to see the connection between the concept or principle and the many applications it may have for our life? We must look beyond the initial explanation, and examine other possible applications. We must look at the similarities in all things. That is not to say we ignore the differences. But noticing similarities, allows our brain to make a comparison to something we can already relate to.

There are usually many different applications for a concept or principle, just as there are usually many different facets of our life that principles can help enhance.

Let's take a look at a symbol that many people are familiar with, but truly do not understand all its implications.

The yin-yang symbol can be seen everywhere you look. It has been used in logos, on book covers, T-shirts, skateboards, in the martial arts, as well as in many other applications. The symbol is said to date back to the fourth century B.C., and has been used by the philosophical religions of Buddhism, Confucianism, and Taoism.

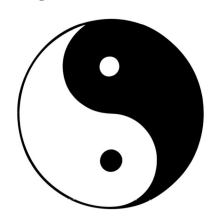

The Yin-Yang represents two opposite, conflicting forces, which blend and coexist in the same space. These forces are found in every action. The symbol is also a reflection of the fact that all things in life are subject to change. The only thing we can be sure of is that life, as we know it today, will change. It is really up to us to try to change things for the better.

The symbol is made up of two teardrops, like halves that seemingly blend into one another. The black portion is Yang, representing such characteristics as hard, forceful, or an outward projection of energy. The white portion is Yin, representative of such characteristics as soft, yielding, or an inward collection of energy. Inside each of the spheres is contained a small seed or portion of the other.

This signifies that whether you are predominately a Yang person, or a Yin person, we all have a small percentage of the qualities from the other.

We can look at this symbol and it's representations in many ways. It can take on the meaning of the balance between FULL and EMPTY. This comparison can be related to characteristics of the human ego; if we are too full of ourselves, we allow ourselves to be closed off to new perspectives and ideas. This makes it very difficult for proper learning and positive growth for the future. On the other hand, if we are too empty, we may accept all perspectives and ideas without questioning whether that particular information is good for us.

Another way of interpreting the yin-yang symbol would be the comparison of being FORCEFUL or YIELDING. There are times in our martial arts where we must be forceful; use of power, speed, and an indomitable spirit to move straight ahead is essential. But as we become more experienced, the realization that having the ability to be yielding, and elusive is equally important.

The important concept to grasp is knowing when and where to apply each quality. Knowing how to use this concept in your daily life is essential when dealing with the conflicts of everyday life.

Yet another comparison of this symbol can be that of the use of STRENGTH and COMPASSION. It is very important in life, to have strength. Strength in your convictions, state of mind, and in your physical sense, is very important for your survival. But being strong without compassion, and an open mind for understanding the people and circumstances around us, can leave us empty and out of balance. As martial artists and students of life, we must have the strength and fierceness of a lion, but, just as importantly, that strength must be tempered by compassion for all those around us.

As we look at these comparisons of the Yin-Yang symbol—and there are countless more—we should start to see a common thread: the pursuit of balance. All of these characteristics from this symbol are very important unto themselves. But mastering the ability to use them in a balanced, productive, and compassionate manner is what a student of the martial arts, and a student of life should strive for.

Rules/Guidelines for Life

As we progress in our training, and become aware of martial arts principles and concepts, we should start to notice how we are governed by natural law. These laws govern how we move, giving us a road map if you will, to better balance and structure as well as ease in movement. Knowing how these concepts/principles apply to us, for better structure and movement, also teaches us the keys of destruction when it comes to our opponent.

When it comes to physically applying our martial arts techniques, we can violate these principles sometimes, depending on our age (youth), strength, and speed. But as we get older, we have to grow smarter and more perceptive to the keys that make our purpose easier, and our opponent's purpose more difficult. If we choose to ignore the fact that these guidelines exist, we are doomed to fail, especially after our physical skills start to diminish.

As we have discussed earlier, principles that govern or relate to physical movement and motion, have a direct relationship in dealing with the mental and emotional challenges of daily living.

Keeping this in mind, I have tried to come up with several simple, straight-forward principles or rules to help guide us when dealing with conflict...physical or non-physical.

1) Pick Your Battles!

Ever feel that you are surrounded by battles/conflicts that constantly require your energy and urgent attention? Sometimes in life, we are drawn into a conflict without our total awareness. Other times, we may dive right in to a fight, without considering the consequences of participating in the conflict. How much time, emotional and physical energy will we have to invest?

Will this sacrifice be beneficial to the betterment of our lives in the long run? Have we looked at the possible outcomes of this situation or conflict? How will our lives, and the lives of those around us, benefit if we prevail? Will there actually be any benefits? Have we considered the down side of engaging in this conflict if we do not prevail? What will we lose, and more importantly, can we afford the loss? Is the fight worth the consequences?

These are all considerations that have to be taken into account, BEFORE we enter into a conflict. In war, just as in daily life, there are never any shortages of conflicts or battles we may engage in. The important thing to remember is that to be an effective and victorious warrior, we must look at the big picture and ask ourselves these important questions. Have we entered into a conflict merely because of our ego, or is the process or fight a worthwhile cause, which will affect you and others in a positive manner?

Always remember, in many cases, we have the opportunity to pick the battles we engage in. But, if we choose not to ask ourselves the important questions, we will find ourselves drawn into conflicts and situations that are not worthy of our time, energy, and possibility of sacrifice and loss.

This guideline is, in no way meant to influence the reader to be totally passive, and to not engage in a conflict. It is merely meant to induce this thought, more often than not we have a choice in the matter. Always remember, when we have a choice, we must evaluate the situation in an objective, educated manner.

2) It is Always Easier to Get Into a Battle or Conflict, Than It is to Get Out!

This guideline goes hand-in-hand with PICK YOUR BATTLES. We have all been drawn into situations, where we've engaged in a conflict, whether it is an argument, legal battle, or dispute of some kind, only to realize the objective is not worth the price we must pay to accomplish it. If we lose the taste for the battle, we may find ourselves wondering how we got involved.

When considering the first guideline, Pick Your Battles, we must consider the fact that the conflict may draw on much longer, and become more costly, than anticipated. This factor must be a major consideration. Are we willing to endure a long, drawn out, mentally and physically draining campaign? If we look back in history, many times we've found ourselves as a country, involved in campaigns that have continued on much longer and become more costly than anticipated. Is the objective worth the sacrifice?

We must look at the conflict and how to appropriately deal with it. Consider all scenarios... What is your exit strategy? Do you have one? At what point would you consider cutting your losses and remove yourself from the conflict?

3) Know Who You're Dealing With!

In the martial sense, this would more appropriately be termed, Know Your Enemy. Since these guidelines are meant to cover a broad spectrum of conflicts or battles which may come our way, we will use, Know Who You're Dealing With. In any interaction with people, there is a certain possibility of conflict. As discussed before, everyone has a certain amount of internal conflict. Therefore, when interacting with others, opinions and viewpoints will often differ, bringing conflict to the surface.

In order to plan out a strategy to avoid conflict, we must know as much as possible about the person or persons we have interactions with. This may be an adversary in business, a neighbor, a co-worker, a spouse, or anyone whom we have some type of relationship with.

First of all, knowing a great deal about the people we interact with, gives us a better understanding of them. We start to see and understand their values and priorities, which guide or drive their behavior. Understanding what things are important and fulfilling to them, allows us to create a more harmonious and balanced relationship with them.

Here are several important characteristics to remember that will help better understand people and why they do what they do.

- *The number-one fear all people have is rejection.*
- *ALL people need to feel accepted by those around them.*
- *Everyone approaches situations with some concern about what's in it for them.*
- *When negotiating or dealing with someone, you must do it in a way that protects or enhances their self-esteem.*
- *People will hear and adopt only concepts that they understand, and can relate to.*
- *People believe and trust those who like them, and share things in common with them.*

Take a look at these guidelines, and see if they don't give you a better understanding of how and why people act.

Knowing these characteristics of the way humans function, and implementing them into your strategy when interacting with others, will change the way you see and deal with other people. This allows us to better avoid conflict and if conflict occurs, allows for better communication and negotiation. Everyone desires to feel important in some way, and wants to feel as though they're being understood. If you make it a constant practice to observe the people around you, and better understand what makes them unique, you will be much more successful in having balanced relationships with them.

4) It's Not Always What You Say, but More Importantly, How You Say It!

Quite often, the delivery of the message is more important than its content. When we are involved in discussions with people, our intent is usually to get the other party to see our viewpoint.

They may feel defensive, or intimidated by our perspective. We may experience feelings of frustration, anger, or impatience, which can cause us to lose sight of our objective. If we do this, our delivery of the message can create a breakdown in the lines of communication. This in turn, makes our objective much more difficult, if not impossible. Remember, that our objective is to win the battle without a fight.

If the delivery of the message is done without the presence of ego, and is done in a manner that allows the other party to see that both sides share common values and interests, communication and resolve of the conflict will take place much quicker. This allows for the feeling of connection with people. Most people will be much more inclined to listen to someone, who they feel understands their interests and concerns.

Sometimes, we allow our emotions to negatively effect our presentation or delivery. If we are feeling emotions of anger or frustration, we may come off as gruff and unconcerned for anyone else's feelings or viewpoints. This usually will result in a much more difficult resolution of the conflict. That's not to say that sometimes our emotions cannot propel us and gives us the ability to deliver a commanding, inspirational message. Sometimes anger and the show of force can be a powerful tool when it comes to an adversary that only understands that mentality.

As you can see, this guideline is directly related to Know Who You're Dealing With. When you better understand the person you're dealing with, the delivery of you're message can be incredibly more effective! When it comes to our emotions, we must choose which emotions are proper for the situation, and use them in a balanced manner. There's that concept of balance, again! Yet it's NOT the easiest thing to do, is it?

5) Take What You Do Seriously...Don't Take Yourself Seriously!

Having an over abundance of ego and self-righteousness can, and usually does end up in the destruction of ourselves, and greatly impairs our relationships with others. Have you ever known someone who was extremely passionate and skilled in what they did, while maintaining a humble attitude about themselves? Their dedication and enthusiasm for what they do is an inspiration to those around them. Their humility creates a feeling of approachability and comfort, which draws people to them.

As people are drawn towards this person, they may pass along compliments and share their admiration. They may comment on this person's incredible level of skill, or their vast knowledge in a given area, in turn putting this person on a pedestal. This is great feedback for the individual, for it gives them the ability to see they're making progress and that they are delivering a quality service.

It is a wonderful thing to be able to feel we are giving good direction to others who share our interest. This is an important process in the development of this leader. Unfortunately, the drawback to this can be that even those who start out as the most humble can start to take these compliments, and themselves, way too seriously. It is easy to forget where we came from; we may forget that we are no better than them, just perhaps further along on the journey than they may be.

If we allow others to feed our ego to the point we take ourselves too seriously, we forget about being compassionate towards others. We lose touch with doing the best we can do, so others can't benefit from our presence. Many great people have fallen because they allow themselves to believe they're larger than life. Take what you do very seriously...but always be careful to NOT take yourself too seriously.

That's why it is so very important to always remain a student. We must strive for continual growth and evolution in what we do, and in who we are.

A very important part of this growth has to come from having a good teacher. As we become more successful in life, we must always remember where we came from. If we, as teachers, forget what it was like when we were white belts, then we cannot relate to the student, and what they need. We must remember the humbling experiences we had when starting this journey.

The importance of having a teacher cannot be overlooked! A good teacher provides guidance to keep us on track. They have traveled this path before us, and can therefore guide us through the pitfalls that lay before us. If our ego needs to be put in check, they provide lessons on humility, when the need arises.

We should be humbled by our teachers in several ways. We should be humbled by our teacher's knowledge and skill of the martial arts. As importantly though, we should be humbled by their actions, personal humility and philosophy. Remember that no one is perfect, and even the best instructors have faults. The key, I guess is...are we working at resolving our issues, and working at bettering ourselves and those around us? Remember to always have the ability to laugh at yourself. TAKE WHAT YOU DO SERIOUSLY, NOT YOURSELF!

6) Take Time to Appreciate What You Have In Your Life.

This guideline is to help us understand and learn to appreciate people and things, we have in our life...while they are here. Too often in life, we get caught up in the busy days, the stress, and the deadlines and commitments we face. We have a tendency to lose sight of what's truly important in our lives. As this happens, people and things in our life begin to drift away, or start to deteriorate. So periodically we must take an inventory of the people, and things in our lives that make us happy and contribute to who we are. We have to pay attention to the action needed to maintain and nurture our relationships, and important components of our life. This could apply to a spouse, loved one, or friend. It could also be a business, a career, or the pursuit of something like the martial arts. As with anything important, there must be a certain amount of dedication, in order to have them continue to be an important, enriching part of our lives.

CHAPTER 4

The Sho Chiku Bai Crest

The Family Crest

The family crest of the art of Kosho Ryu Kempo, is called the Sho Chiku Bai Mon. This crest contains many of the keys that contribute to a well-rounded study of both life and the martial arts. The Sho Chiku Bai Mon has elements that are approximately 750 years old. Mon Gaku or the study of the Sho Chiku Bai crest, gives the student insights into the spiritual and philosophical studies, as well as the physical studies.

Study of the philosophical arts, the most important study, gives practitioners insights into how to keep themselves in check with their surroundings and teaches them how to blend with their environment, and be a positive contributor to society. The three interpretations of the Mon are as follows: the spiritual and philosophical study, the physical study, and the study of the destructive arts.

Let's dissect the crest and identify and explain its components.

Starting from the outside of the crest, we see the circle surrounding it. The circle represents totality – maybe a journey, or a learning experience that has come full circle, that has led a practitioner to a deeper understanding. Maybe it's a reminder that we need to always be well rounded in our practices, keeping an open mind to new ideas and perspectives, thus allowing growth in our lives.

Next, we have the eight angles of the octagon. The octagon is the most important aspect of the study of the physical arts.

The Eightfold Path

The first representation of the eight angles is the Eightfold Path of Buddhism. The Eightfold Path can be compared to the Ten Commandments of Christianity. The purpose of the Ten Commandments is to educate the practitioner in what actions are not appropriate. The Eightfold Path, educates the practitioner in what actions are appropriate. These actions are as follows:

1) *Right Speech*—We need to choose our words wisely. We need to consider to whom we are speaking, including their perspectives and viewpoints. Right speech creates harmony, while improper speech creates conflict and disharmony. Always remember...it's not always what we say, but more importantly, how we say it!

2) *Right Understanding*—We must take the time to understand ourselves, and the people around us. The more we know about the people we're dealing or interacting with, the easier it is to understand them. We need to understand their values, perspectives, and priorities since this forms the core of their behavioral attributes.

3) *Right Means of Livelihood*—We all need to make a living, to financially support ourselves and our families. As important as it is to financially support ourselves, we must also remember that the means we use to accomplish this must be in line with the laws and guidelines set forth by society. If we stay within these laws, we contribute to that society. If we violate these laws, by using improper means to support ourselves, we create disharmony and cause harm.

4) *Right Effort*—Having the attitude of doing everything to the best of our abilities or capabilities sends a message about us. This mindset tells people around us that we are humble, conscientious, hard-working, focused, and dedicated in all aspects of our lives. These areas include our work, our personal and professional lives, as well as our martial arts training.

5) *Right Meditation*—Meditation can be interpreted many different ways. One aspect of this is a better understanding of how to become more centered and focused individuals. The process of meditation should enable the practitioner calm and cleanse the mind while energizing internally, thereby allowing us to view our environment in a much clearer, more objective manner. This process should allow us to be more receptive to our instincts and inner wisdom. Meditation should also be a tool to help us to slow down and learn to appreciate the moment. Live the philosophy of life in every breath.

6) *Right Action*—Life rewards action! Intentions are important, but people generally don't care about your intention. They care about what you do! They don't really care what you meant to do! Words are easy, action is difficult. As we move forward on our journey, we must make careful, well-informed decisions—then pull the trigger, and act on them. All of this must be with the right purpose in mind. Our actions should always have a mutual benefit for the betterment of ourselves, and for all other parties involved. Our actions should be taken with the intent to create harmony for ourselves and everyone in our environment. Be a person of planned, educated action performed for the right purpose.

7) *Right Intention*—The use of proper motives or intentions in our endeavors is critical to creating and maintaining harmony in our lives. Intentions are the precursor for action. They

must fuel the fire for our actions. These intentions must be in line with what is for our better-ment, and that of everyone involved. Also, in keeping with the thought that we should have a keen awareness of what is going on around us, we need to explore other people's intentions. Understand what their underlying motives may be. What's in it for them? Do they genuinely have our best interests in mind? Always analyze others' intentions, as well as your own.

8) *Right Awareness*—Having proper awareness of our environment and ourselves is vital to dealing with life in a preparatory manner, allowing us to see situations and circumstances as they develop. Being aware of ourselves and how we fit into our surroundings gives us insights into creating harmony within that environment. Proper awareness is the cornerstone of effec-tive self-defense, protecting oneself from potential physical harm from another individual, or avoidance of any situation that is detrimental to our well-being. Be aware of people and their motivations, both good and bad, and gain insight into what drives them. Then, and only then, can we make a judgment as to whether such a relationship is beneficial to our lives.

The Eight Fold Path gives us a guide for the betterment of the self and the community. It holds the keys to blending with others, and avoidance of unwanted conflict, to aid in creating a more enjoyable, fulfilling life.

Eight Aspects of Study

The second representation of the octagon involves the eight angles that signify the different areas of Kempo study, which a student should pursue.

Angle #1–Energy Collection

Energy Collection includes, but is not limited to, the study of breath, posture, triangulation of alignments, timing, visualization, energy gathering and projection, kata, kumite, and bunkai.

Angle #2–Healing Arts

Healing Arts include, but are not limited to, the study of the Five Element Theory, anatomy, physiology, body systems, shiatsu, anma, nutrition, herbology, the study of boshin, bunshin, munshin, setsushin (all diagnostic techniques), posture, energy projection and gathering, kata, kumite, and bunkai.

Angle #3–Japanese Yoga

Japanese Yoga includes, but is not limited to, the study of stretching and conditioning ex-ercises designed specifically for the study of Kosho Ryu martial arts, as well as for general fitness, breathing, posture, triangulation of alignments, timing, visualization, energy gathering and projection, kata, kumite, and bunkai.

Angle #4–Escaping Arts

Escaping Arts include, but are not limited to, the study of breathing, posture, natural move-ment, triangulation of alignments, timing, jumping patterns, angling, eye training with respect to reducing negative stimuli to reaction time, falling techniques, hearing arts and the reading of the opponent's intent, the study of metabolism, kata, kumite, and bunkai.

Angle #5–Philosophy

Philosophy includes, but is not limited to, the study of the Mon, and of culture, history, and awareness of the physical self along with awareness of the spiritual self, kata, kumite, and bunkai.

Angle #6–Folding Arts

Folding Arts include, but are not limited to, the study of fundamental throwing techniques, fundamental releasing techniques, fundamental ground techniques, breathing, leverage, anatomy, natural movement, entering motion, engagement and disengagement with a moving opponent, kyo and jitsu, kata, kumite, and bunkai.

Angle #7–Meditation

Meditation includes, but is not limited to the study of Shodo (Japanese Brush Calligraphy), Ikebana (Japanese Flower Arranging), Iaido (Swordsmanship practice for the sharpening of the mind and spirit), comprehensive understanding of philosophy and energy collection, history, understanding of kokoro, kime (focus), kata, kumite, and bunkai.

Angle #8–The War Arts

War Arts include, but are not limited to, the study of strategy, timing, posture and positioning, angling, combative distancing, Kenjutsu (Japanese fencing), Iaijutsu (swordsmanship with combat application done from the sheathed position), Naginatajutsu (Halberd arts), Sojutsu (Spearmanship), Bojutsu (long staff arts), Jojutsu (short staff arts), Tantojutsu (knife arts), natural movement, vital point striking, skeletal striking, nerve striking, internal striking, breathing, triangulation of alignments, energy gathering and projection exercises, kata, kumite, and bunkai.

Sho Chiku Bai

Next we will look at the elements pictured within the octagon of the crest.

Pine, Bamboo, Plum Blossom

Sho (Matsuda)–Pine

Evergreens live long, young, and healthy lives. The Pine symbolizes faithful friendship that resists all trials. The pine represents the religion of Taoism. The Japanese people use pine needles for ornaments on Christmas and New Year.

Chiku (Take)–Bamboo

Bamboo represents honesty. When you cut into bamboo, you find emptiness inside. Nothing evil is hidden within. A good Kosho Ryu student remains ever empty, and always open to additional knowledge, never becoming full of themselves and their accomplishments. The bamboo is the symbol of the application of discipline, and the man who remains loyal in all events. Bamboo represents the Japanese religion of Buddhism.

Bai (Baika)–Plum Flower

The Japanese plum flower stands for beauty, nobility, and courage. This is because the plum flower puts forth blossoms while the snow is on the ground. The plum tree flowers before all of the others. The Japanese people love the plum fruit, eating them especially when they are sick. The plum represents the Japanese religion of Shintoism.

The Hand Postures

Kigan–Praying Hands Position

First Representation: The right hand (representing the physical) and the left hand (representing the spiritual) are placed together for peace and avoidance of conflict.

Second Representation: Escaping Arts

Third Representation: Skeletal Strikes

Kaishu–Open Hand Position

First Representation: The right hand and left hand are placed together in the shape of a mountain. One should look for the good in man, as you would see a mountain from a distance, without nitpicking flaws and imperfections.

Second Representation: Folding Arts

Third Representation: Internal Strikes

Hoken–Covered Fist Position

First Representation: The right hand (representing the physical skills) is covered by the left hand (representing the spiritual skills). One should temper his/her actions with morality, avoid conflict, and hide his/her weapons.

Second Representation: Muscular Strikes

Third Representation: Total Domination

CHAPTER 5

The Octagon

The Octagon

The use of the octagon is very important to the student of Kosho Ryu Kempo. Whatever art you study, the concepts of the octagon can enhance your own understanding of what you do. The use of the octagon gives us a tool to practice and understand stances, directional movement, transitional motion, and how to be evasive in our escaping. The ability to escape harm from an opponent, and to do no harm to them, is considered the highest art. When working our escaping on the octagon, we have to understand the relationship of the 12-6-3 theory, and the use of tunnel and peripheral vision. Depending on which visual mode we're using, our reaction time differs, as does the angle of the octagon we use.

Since our reaction time is delayed when we're in tunnel vision mode, we would use different angles of escape, depending on the distance between our opponent and ourselves.

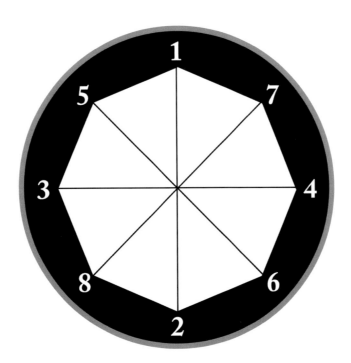

In tunnel vision mode, as an opponent attacks from a distance of 12 feet, we would move to angles #5 or #7.

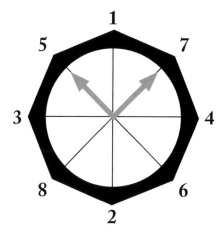

In peripheral vision mode at 12 feet, we can use any angle other than #1, for total escape.

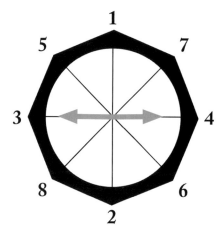

At a distance of 6 feet, using tunnel vision, we would use angles #3 and #4.

At a distance of 6 feet, using peripheral vision, we would use angles #5 and #7

At a distance of 3 feet, using tunnel vision, we would use angles #6 and #8.

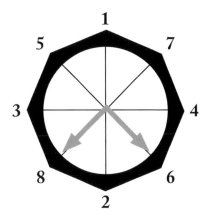

At the same distance of 3 feet, using peripheral vision, our choice would be angles #3 and #4.

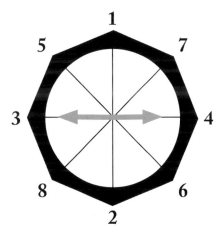

Eight Angles of Escape

The angles of the octagon act as a roadmap, if you will, to give the practitioner directional avenues in which to avoid contact with an opponent. They also allow the practitioner to reposition, to avoid taking on the mass of an opponent.

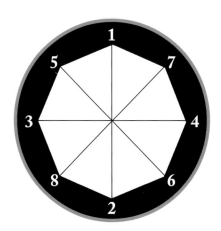

As we look at the octagon angles for the use of escape, we have to ask ourselves whether we are using them for total escape from an attacker, or whether we are looking for momentary repositioning to avoid mass and find a superior angle from which to initiate our attack. This gives us two different attitudes of escape. The first, and most important, would that be that of total avoidance of body contact.

Imagine if you were virtually untouchable! Imagine the confidence you would have. Knowing that no matter what an attacker threw at you, you had the ability to evade any contact. In this instance, we use a total escape attitude of the octagon. View the page on the Octagon for Total Escape for photos.

If we choose to engage our opponent, but do not want to take on their body mass while attaining a superior position to attack from, we must escape and align ourselves for engagement. In doing so, we must position our body in a way that easily allows us to use our intended weapon or weapons for attack (see page on Octagon for Escape & Engagement). For instance, if we choose to attack with a hand combination, we would align our triangles towards the at-

Figure A

Figure B

Figure C

Figure D

tacker. This would give us optimum use of our upper body weapons, for use when the attacker rotates. (Figures A and B) If we choose to attack with a yoko geri, or side kick, we must escape and position that particular weapon for it's use. (Figures C and D)

The Center Pole of the Octagon

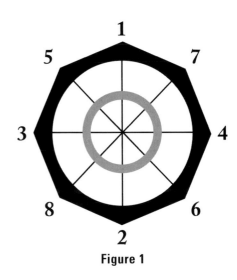

Figure 1

Another very important aspect of the octagon, would be the center pole. The center pole is very important for several reasons.

First of all, the center pole represents the neutral zone between yourself and an attacker. (Figure 1) If you look at the space between yourself and an opponent, you being at angle #2, and the opponent at angle #1, this neutral zone in the middle would be the center pole (Figure 2).

In order for an opponent to grab or hit you, they must occupy or cross this space. Knowing this allows the practitioner to occupy that space, and create a jamming effect as the opponent starts to move forward to attack (Figure 3).

Figure 2

Figure 3

Secondly, manipulation of any incoming strikes or grabs is extremely effective in this area. Blocking or parrying as the opponent settles into a base is less effective because his weight is moving into a downward stabilizing motion.

When we are settled into a base, we must rappel from that stance. The weight has to rise slightly, to move effectively. Our initial rappelling motion is needed to rise to overcome gravity.

So, as the body rises, the practitioner loses the foundation. As a result manipulation of the center and its extremities has a greater effect on his body structure. Therefore, any block or parry done at the area of the center pole will catch the opponent in a weightless state.

Figure 4   **Figure 5**

In Figure 4, the attacker shifts the body weight up and forward, throwing a right punch. The defender moves forward and meets the attacker's punching arm at the center pole of the octagon, disrupting his balance and structure (Figure 5).

The center pole concept is also very useful when dealing with the striking arts. People naturally position themselves with a certain amount of space between themselves and other people. If we understand this, we realize that an opponent has to move in and take up this space, to actually connect with us. So, striking to this neutral space is extremely effective for destruction of the balance and structure of the opponent. Notice how an attacker needs the neutral space between the two of you.

Figure 6   **Figure 7**

In Figure 6, notice the neutral zone between the attacker and the defender. This is the center pole area. When the attacker seeks proper distancing in order to strike, his body will move into the center pole area of the octagon. The defender merely needs to move (avoiding the opponent) and strike to this area, causing the attacker to run into the strike (Figure 7).

As we know, striking an opponent while he is rotating toward his target catches him in a weightless state. Using the center pole concept is especially effective on an attacker's secondary rotation.

Figure 8

Figure 9

In Figure 8, the attacker steps in to throw a right punch, and the defender slips out to angle #3 and parry blocks the punch on an inward angle. This causes the attacker to over-rotate. The defender aligns triangles towards the attacker's center. The attacker will then rotate and move into the area of the center pole. The defender strikes with a male percussion strike, which the attacker runs into (Figure 9).

The center pole concept is also very applicable for the use of joint locks/manipulations. Let's take a basic joint lock; a kotegaeshi or outward wristlock. Apply an outward wristlock on your training partner. Observe the amount of space your arms need to maneuver, to properly apply the lock.

Figure 10

If we look at the positioning needed to apply this lock you will notice that you and your partner are basically at angles #1 and #2. Your hands control and manipulate the wrist joint of your training partner, at the center pole location of the octagon (Figure 10).

Figure 11

Figure 12

If your partner were to reposition his body into the center pole area, you would find yourself jammed and unable to apply the lock, due to lack of maneuverable space (Figure 11). You would need to step back to regain the space required for applying the lock (Figure 12).

Figure 13

Figure 14

Keeping this thought in mind, the practitioner can utilize this application of the octagon for use in countering an opponent's attempted joint lock.

By entering into this space, as your opponent begins to apply the lock, you steal away the area needed to operate effectively (Figure 13 and 14). This creates an imbalance in your opponent's structure, which allows for application of a throwing technique (Figure 15 and 16).

Figure 15

Figure 16

Placement of the Octagon

The octagon can be used in a variety of ways, giving key points of understanding for directional application. This gives the practitioner various alternatives for interaction with an opponent, for most effective escaping, throwing, and striking. The following examples are just some of the ways that the octagon can act as a map for better understanding of movement and motion.

Placing the Octagon On the Floor

First, let's look at the octagon placed on the floor, and the different ways we can apply it. There are several ways we can interpret the octagon placed on the floor. In Figure 17, the attacker is at angle #1 of the octagon, and the defender is at the center pole. From this application, the defender can use all of the angles for either total escape, or escaping and turning into the attacker to engage. Figure 18 shows the defender slipping out to angle #3, and rotating behind his triangles to engage.

Another interpretation of the octagon placed on the floor, would be that of the attacker positioned at angle #1 and the defender positioned at angle #2. In this instance, the defender

Figure 17

Figure 18

would use the center pole of the octagon, as an intercepting point by which to disrupt and manipulate the attacker's aggressive movement (Figures 19 and 20).

Figure 19

Figure 20

Figure 21

Figure 22

If we look at how the body moves, and the angles created as an attacker attempts to strike, we put the attacker at the center pole of the octagon. Placing the attacker in the center of the octagon, notice the various angles the body rotates to, in the process of throwing a strike.

Figure 23

For instance, the body generally starts out with the body squared towards the opponent. This would be angles #3 and #4 as in Figure 21. From this position, the attacker will rock back slightly, as his right hip and shoulder retracts, and the left hip and shoulder projects to angles #5 and #6 (Figure 22). This initial motion is the body cocking, so it may rotate and generate power on the strike.

As the attacker rappels from this cocked position, he will retract the left hip and shoulder, and project his right hip and shoulder, to strike through the target. This puts his body position at angles #7 and #8 (Figure 23).

Observe how the body repositions and rotates. Notice what angles the body moves to. Look at the similarities of motion when the octagon is utilized. Notice how the body rappels, moves center, and then settles again to strike. Look at the various angles the body may be manipulated to, through use of checking and freezing. Study all these things then relate them to an opponent's movement, and your movement as well.

Placing the Octagon On the Body

Take the octagon and place it on the body and make note of how it relates to the body. Notice the intersecting points between various body parts and the angles of the octagon. The shoulders, hips, and knees, and center, all have a relationship to these angles.

Take this upright octagon and place it between yourself and your opponent. Use the octagon in this context, to guide the opponent's incoming weapon to a desired angle. Notice the effects that are created on the body. Look for the folds this may create.

Observe how parrying or manipulating the incoming punch or grab to these angles causes the body to over rotate. This places the opponent in a difficult position when he readjusts to throw a follow-up strike. Notice how this may set-up the opponent for various striking or throwing techniques. Now view how this octagon can assist you when dealing with an opponent who has applied a grab. Notice how when you are grabbed creasing the elbow to different angles of the octagon causes different folds and creases. These folds and creases will help set-up various throws, locks, and striking techniques. Experiment with placement of the octagon, and observe!

Octagon Kata & Drills

In the following pages, we will show some of the kata, and basic drills for use with the octagon, which will enhance the student's understanding and use of the octagon. These are by no means the only kata or drills by which the octagon can be studied. Many practitioners will start with these drills, only to see other interpretations as their study deepens. Notice how the use of the octagon can be incorporated into your studies – no matter what art you study.

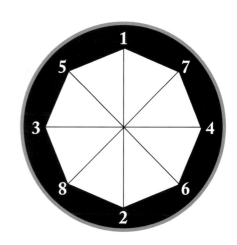

The basic octagon kata has several uses. First a student must concentrate on developing good basic fundamentals. Performance of the octagon kata will enhance the practitioner's basic stances, blocking and striking, as well as a basic understanding of the octagon and its angles. On the following pages we will demonstrate octagon kata in front stance (zenkutsu dachi) and in back stance (kokutsu dachi).

Octagon Zenkutsu Dachi

Octagon Zenkutsu Dachi Angle #1

Starting from the center of the octagon, from a parallel stance, or heiko dachi, the practitioner raises the arms to cover center.

The practitioner then steps forward with the left foot (foot is placed between angles #5 & #1), moving center to angle #1, into a front leaning stance, or zenkutsu dachi.

After settling in the front stance, execute a low level sweeping block, or gedan barai.

The practitioner then rappels from the front stance, back to a parallel stance, at the center of the octagon.

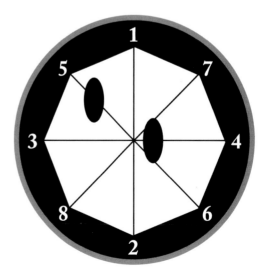

Octagon Zenkutsu Dachi Angle #2

Starting from the center of the octagon, from a parallel stance, or heiko dachi, the practitioner raises the arms to cover center.

The practitioner then steps back with the left foot (foot is placed between angles #8 & #2), moving the center back to angle #2, into a front leaning stance, or zenkutsu dachi.

After settling into the front stance, execute a low-level sweeping block, gedan barai.

The practitioner then rappels from the front stance, back to a parallel stance, at the center of the octagon.

Octagon Zenkutsu Dachi Angle #3

Starting from the center of the octagon, from a parallel stance, or heiko dachi, the practitioner raises the arms to cover center.

The practitioner then steps back and to the left, with the left foot (foot is placed between angles #3 & #8), turning center to angle #3, into a front leaning stance, or zenkutsu dachi.

After settling in the front stance, execute a low level sweeping block, or gedan barai.

The practitioner then rappels from the front stance, back to a parallel stance, at the center of the octagon.

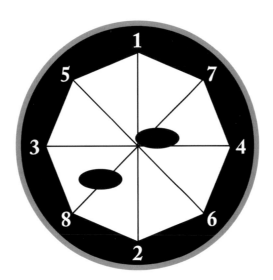

Octagon Zenkutsu Dachi Angle #4

Starting from the center of the octagon, from a parallel stance, or heiko dachi, the practitioner raises the arms to cover center.

The practitioner then steps back and to the right, with the right foot (foot is placed between angles #4 & #6), turning center to angle #4, into a front leaning stance, or zenkutsu dachi.

After settling in the front stance, execute a low level sweeping block, or gedan barai.

The practitioner then rappels from the front stance, back to a parallel stance, at the center of the octagon.

Octagon Zenkutsu Dachi Angle #5

Starting from the center of the octagon, from a parallel stance, or heiko dachi, the practitioner raises the arms to cover center.

The practitioner steps out with the left foot (foot is placed between angles #5 & #3), turning center to angle #5, settling into a front leaning stance, or zenkutsu dachi.

The practitioner then executes a low-level sweeping block, or gedan barai, with the left arm.

The practitioner then rappels from the front stance, back to a parallel stance, at the center of the octagon.

Octagon Zenkutsu Dachi Angle #6

Starting from the center of the octagon, from a parallel stance, or heiko dachi, the practitioner raises the arms to cover center.

The practitioner pivots the right foot. and steps back with the left foot, placing it between angles #2 & #6, settling into a front stance or zenkutsu dachi.

The practitioner then executes a low-level sweeping block, or gedan barai, with the right arm.

The practitioner then rappels from the front stance, back to a parallel stance, at the center of the octagon.

Octagon Zenkutsu Dachi Angle #7

Starting from the center of the octagon, from a parallel stance, or heiko dachi, the practitioner raises the arms to cover center.

The practitioner steps out with the right foot (foot is placed between angles #7 & #4), moving center to angle #7, settling into a front leaning stance, or zenkutsu dachi.

The practitioner then executes a low-level sweeping block, or gedan barai, with the right arm.

The practitioner then rappels from the front stance, back to a parallel stance at the center of the octagon.

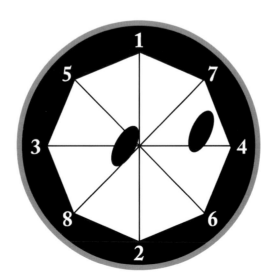

Octagon Zenkutsu Dachi Angle #8

Starting from the center of the octagon, from a parallel stance, or heiko dachi, the practitioner raises the arms to cover center.

The practitioner pivots the left foot and steps back with the right foot, placing it between angles #2 & #8, settling into a front stance or zenkutsu dachi.

The practitioner then executes a low-level sweeping block, or gedan barai, with the left arm.

The practitioner then rappels from the front stance, back to a parallel stance, at the center of the octagon.

Octagon Kokutsu Dachi

Octagon Kokutsu Dachi Angle #1

Starting from the center of the octagon, from a parallel stance, or heiko dachi, the practitioner raises the arms to cover center.

The practitioner steps forward with the left foot in kokutsu dachi, or back stance, while moving his center to angle #1.

He then executes a left shuto, or knife hand strike.

The practitioner then rappels from the back stance, to a parallel stance, at the center of the octagon.

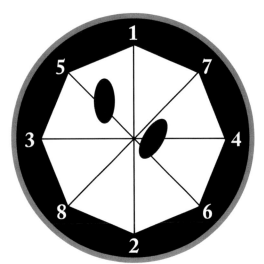

Octagon Kokutsu Dachi Angle #2

Starting from the center of the octagon, from a parallel stance, or heiko dachi, the practitioner raises the arms to cover center.

The practitioner steps back with the left foot in kokutsu dachi, or back stance, while moving his center to angle #2.

He then executes a right shuto, or knife hand strike.

The practitioner then rappels from the back stance, to a parallel stance, at the center of the octagon.

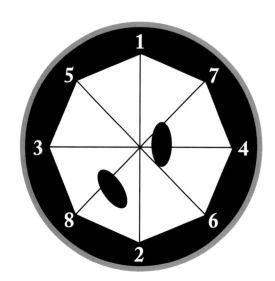

Octagon Kokutsu Dachi Angle #3

Starting from the center of the octagon, from a parallel stance, or heiko dachi, the practitioner raises the arms to cover center.

The practitioner steps out to angle #3, with the left foot, into a kokutsu dachi, or back stance.

He then executes a left shuto, or knife hand to angle #3.

The practitioner then rappels from the back stance, to a parallel stance, at the center of the octagon.

Octagon Kokutsu Dachi Angle #4

Starting from the center of the octagon, from a parallel stance, or heiko dachi, the practitioner raises the arms to cover center.

The practitioner steps out to angle #4, with the right foot, into a kokutsu dachi, or back stance.

He then executes a right shuto, or knife hand to angle #4.

The practitioner then rappels from the back stance, to a parallel stance, at the center of the octagon.

Octagon Kokutsu Dachi Angle #5

Starting from the center of the octagon, from a parallel stance, or heiko dachi, the practitioner raises the arms to cover center.

The practitioner steps with the left foot, out to angle #5, into a kokutsu dachi, or back stance.

He then executes a left shuto, or knife hand.

The practitioner then rappels from the back stance, to a parallel stance, at the center of the octagon.

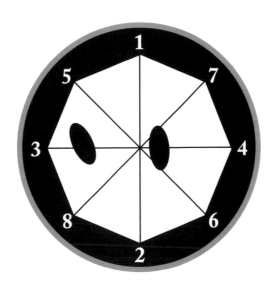

Octagon Kokutsu Dachi Angle #6

Starting from the center of the octagon, from a parallel stance, or heiko dachi, the practitioner raises the arms to cover center.

The practitioner steps back with the left foot to angle #6, into a kokutsu dachi or back stance.

He then executes a right shuto, or knife hand. Center is facing angle #5.

The practitioner then rappels from the back stance, to a parallel stance, at the center of the octagon.

Octagon Kokutsu Dachi Angle #7

Starting from the center of the octagon, from a parallel stance, or heiko dachi, the practitioner raises the arms to cover center.

The practitioner steps with the right foot, out to angle #7, into a kokutsu dachi, or back stance.

He then executes a right shuto, or knife hand.

The practitioner then rappels from the back stance, to a parallel stance, at the center of the octagon.

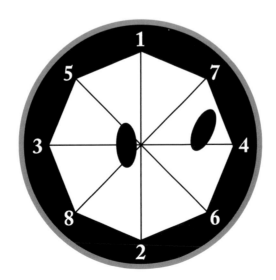

Octagon Kokutsu Dachi Angle #8

Starting from the center of the octagon, from a parallel stance, or heiko dachi, the practitioner raises the arms to cover center.

The practitioner steps back with the right foot to angle #8, into a kokutsu dachi or back stance.

He then executes a left shuto, or knife hand. Center is facing angle #7.

The practitioner then rappels from the back stance, to a parallel stance, at the center of the octagon.

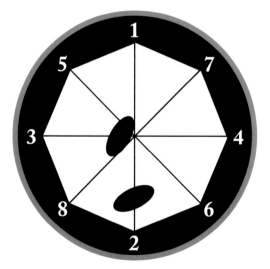

Practice the preceding octagon kata using zenkutsu dachi (front stance) and kokutsu dachi (back stance). Start from the center of the octagon, moving your center to the direction of the intended angle of the octagon. After settling into the stance, return to a parallel stance in the center of the octagon. Notice the muscle groups that must initiate the motion to propel the body in the proper direction.

Observe and feel lower body manipulations that will enhance your transitional motion, from one step to the next.

Next, perform the same drill, this time working two angles together.

Angles #1 & #2

Starting position at the center of the octagon

 Step with the left foot and move your center to angle #1, into a front stance and execute a down block. Immediately after settling into the stance and performing the block, bring arms in to cover center and rappel from the stance, initiating the motion to move to the back angle.

 Finish by stepping back with the left foot, moving your center back to angle #2.

 Rappel from the stance at angle #2, pushing the body back to a parallel stance at the center of the octagon.

Angles #3 & #4

Starting at the neutral position in the center of the octagon, bring the arms up to cover center, as the left footsteps back to angle #8.

Rotate center to angle #3, and execute a low block.

Bring the arms in to cover center, left (rear) leg steps across to angle #6.

Rotate center around to angle #4, and execute a low block.

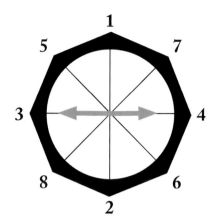

Angles #5 & #6

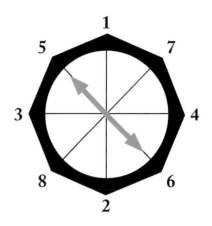

Rappel from that stance back to neutral position facing angle #1.

Bring the arms up to cover center, left footsteps out between angles #3 and #5, and rotate center to angle #5 as you execute a low block.

Rappel from this stance as you bring the arms in to cover center, as you rappel from the front stance with the left foot, moving back through the center pole.

Continue this motion, bringing the left foot back and placing between angles #2 & #6, settling into a right foot forward front stance. Align center to angle #5 and execute a right low block.

Angles #7 & #8

Rappel back to neutral stance facing angle #1.

Step with right foot out between angles #7 & #4, while aligning center to angle #7. Execute a right low block.

Rappel from this stance, bringing right leg back through the center pole area, as the arms come in to cover center.

Continue this motion back, setting the right foot down between angles #8 & #2 into a left foot forward front stance. Align center towards angle #7 and execute a left low block.

Return to the center pole area of the octagon, in a neutral stance, facing angle #1.

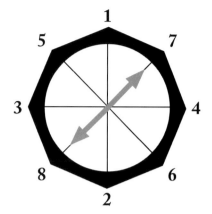

This same kata should also be done using kokutsu dachi, sanchin dachi, and neko ashi dachi. As the practitioner is practicing these kata, take note of the muscle groups that energize or tense, to initiate the next movement. Also note how the feet make natural adjustments, setting or loading up, to propel the body.

There is a wealth of information to be gained by studying and working with the octagon. As you study, you will see various applications that will enhance your training. Take your time, observe movement and motion, and apply it to your martial arts training, and apply it to your daily life.

Octagon for Total Escape

Octagon for Escape & Engagement

CHAPTER 6

Concepts of Study

Concepts

As we go through life, we start to notice that there is something deeper to what we do. We come to a realization that there are principles all around us, whether it be philosophical principles which guide us in daily life, or martial principles that allow us to execute a technique with less effort and more economy of motion. Whether we admit it or not, the fact is we are governed by these principles. You can deny this, only to feel that you seem to force your way through life and feel as though there is resistance to everything you do. Do you ever feel this way? Of course, we all do from time to time.

As a member of society, laws that establish boundaries of action and behavior govern us. These laws/principles of society are put into place to keep balance and harmony among individuals in a community. If we break these laws/principles, there are consequences we must face.

In your martial arts, these concepts/principles are there for much the same reason; to guide you and allow you to perform your art with balance and harmony, blending with your opponent and flowing with whatever comes your way. In life, when we are in a balanced and proper frame of mind, things seem to flow and fall into place without an excess of effort and stress. Our performance of our martial art should be no exception.

But the nagging question seems to be: How do we arrive at this point? How do we start to notice and understand these concepts? Obviously, there is a process to this, just as in life. It is a journey, one for which a guide is very necessary. We can go through life learning the HARD way, or we can pay attention our teachers/guides for the insights that will enhance our journey, making it a smoother, more enjoyable process. Children come into this world and set out on their journey of development. They are guided and taught by their parents, schoolteachers and mentors along the way. These guides/ teachers are there to awaken us all to things that are not readily seen, helping us grow and gain an understanding of life and its lessons.

Each of these teachers has gone through the same process before us. In the martial sense, we make up our mind to learn the basic fundamentals of the art. Then we must perform countless repetitions to internalize them. Then finally, the student will start to see underlying concepts that govern these motions and provide options for different applications. This process must be done under the watchful eye of a good teacher, pointing out the necessary lessons and principles along the way as the student becomes ready. The teacher is there to guide and point out things to make the students' journey productive and to assist them through the pitfalls of their training, as well as humble them when needed.

Yet it is not enough to have a good teacher. The student must be a willing participant in this relationship. A good student must first have two things: trust and faith. The student must trust that the instructor's demands are in his best interest. The student must also have faith that the instructor will teach him the proper information at the proper time in his development. An experienced instructor knows what information a student is ready for, and when they will be prepared to accept it.

We've all heard the saying "When the student is ready, the teacher will appear." What does that mean? This can have several meanings. First of all, the student may be searching for something in particular. As the student begins to realize what qualities and qualifications are needed, doors will open and eventually he will find the teacher needed to fulfill these needs. Secondly, we can look at the notion that the information can be the teacher. Even as the student is exposed to it, he may not be at a developmental stage in which he will be able to understand and appreciate it. Yet another way of looking at this would be to realize that sometimes we must also act as our own teacher. By this I mean we must perform countless repetitions and begin to look deeper into things. We must ask questions, study the teachings of great masters, and develop an eye for watching our teachers' movements, attitudes, and the feeling they project when demonstrating. So remember: "When the student is ready, the teacher will appear."

In the following pages of this chapter, we will be looking at concepts that can lead to a deeper understanding of any style of martial art. You may ask; "How can principles or concepts from Kosho Ryu Kempo help with my art?" The reality is, these concepts are not unique just to Kosho Ryu Kempo. Kempo is a study, not a style. These principles are based on natural laws, which governs movement and motion, and therefore governs all martial arts.

These concepts/principles exist in every art form. They are observations of people involved in study, who have looked deeper into what they do. Different people have said many of the things said in this book before, in different ways. The words in this book are merely my interpretation of information that has been passed on to me. Information can take on many different meanings or interpretations, depending on the individual, his/her experience, and where he or she is on the path of this journey.

As you study the following pages, look deeply into what you read. Look at how it applies to your martial study. Then look at how the principle or concept can apply to your personal and professional life. Look for the similarities in your martial art and your daily life. Let the concepts allow you to see things from a different perspective, and above all else, enjoy the process or the journey.

In the next few sections we will delve into some of these natural laws and principles.

The Leaning Factor

The leaning factor relates to a natural motion that takes place when someone wants to move from one posture to another.

For instance, in order to take a step, the body must shift the weight to one of the feet in order to take a step or reposition the other foot. This is the natural process of walking we all do without thinking about it. In the martial sense, by using the leaning factor we are using a preparatory motion to adjust our weight in advance of the attack. Kosho Ryu is an art that is preparatory in nature instead of reactionary. In an art that is reactionary, the defender would (without thinking) take this action when they see the attack beginning, therefore making it more difficult to move on time.

In Kosho Ryu, the student is trained to create an illusion for his opponent. The leaning factor not only shifts/repositions the weight prior to the attack for ease of movement, but also creates an illusion of where the defender's center is positioned. In a sense, we are baiting the opponent to attack where he perceives our center (his target) to be, when actually we are somewhere else. (Fig. #24 & #25)

Figure 24

Figure 25

Through the process of understanding how the leaning factor enables us to move with ease and proper timing, we must also look at these principles and how they govern our opponent's motion as well.

Realize that the opponent must shift his weight in the opposite direction of the intended attack in order to project his strike. How can we use this information to our benefit?

Perform the following drill: Have your partner throw slow punches at you. You in turn will work your leaning factor (preparatory posturing) and escape to different angles of the octagon each time your partner strikes, staying at medium range distance from your partner. Contact his/her arm or shoulder immediately after avoiding each strike to feel your partner's next motion. Your objective in this drill is to feel how your partner must initially shift his weight for each strike. By performing this drill slowly, you can see and feel that there is a preparatory shift in weight needed to create the ability to strike or grab you. It is very important to recognize this.

Once you are comfortable you can feel this shift, proceed. This time perform the same drill, but escape and maintain a shorter (closer) distance to your partner. After each punch and escape, place your hand lightly on different places of your partner's body. When your partner attempts to strike again, feel for the initial body shift and manipulate/push in that direction. You should be able to put your partner off-balance with a relatively small amount of force. This drill is geared towards developing sensitivity in feeling your partner's preparatory shifting of weight and manipulating him to make his objective more difficult.

Remember to work these drills slowly to observe and gain sensitivity to feel these concepts.

Visual Skills: Peripheral vs. Tunnel Vision

The use of peripheral and tunnel vision and the understanding of when to use each mode of vision are extremely important. For instance, understanding that the use of peripheral vision will allow you to detect motion much more quickly and allow you to move on time.

Why is this possible? The eyes contain rods and cones, which pick up motion, color, shapes and texture. The brain must process this information, so the more detail you are looking for, the longer it takes. Tunnel vision is the mode of vision you would use when you are taking in a great amount of information or require a great deal of focus. Peripheral vision sense shapes and movement but discards much of this detail and therefore registers the image faster.

For instance, if you are looking at a painting, you are taking in the detail of the painting such as color, texture, etc. Your brain is processing this information in order for you to enjoy the painting and get a sense of what the artist meant to relay through his or her work. For this application, tunnel vision is appropriate. You have no immediate need to move or reposition your body in this situation.

On the other hand, peripheral vision does not take in as much detail for the brain to process. In an application where you act or reposition your body, peripheral vision is far superior. If you look at an object peripherally, you are not picking up a great amount of detail, therefore visually picking up motion quicker for you to act and reposition your body.

Try this exercise the next time you are in your car stopped at a red light: Look at the light in tunnel vision mode. You objective is to react to the light changing to green and step on the gas to pull out. Notice the length of reaction time from seeing the light change to stepping on the gas. At the next stoplight, look at the light in peripheral vision mode and again notice the reaction time taken to respond to the changing light. You should notice when using peripheral vision, your reaction time should be greatly reduced.

Another very important aspect of tunnel vision is its tendency to connect or draw you in to whatever you are looking at. For instance, when driving your car into a sharp turn, notice how when you look at the curve instead of looking through the turn, how you seem to be drawn into the turn. If when you drive into a turn, you focus your tunnel vision on looking through the turn, you are not pulled or drawn into the side of the road. So, in a self-defense situation where an attacker is attempting to hit you, looking at him with tunnel vision will actually establish a connection and draw you into him.

Figure 26

Now take this concept and apply it to a training partner punching at you while using tunnel and then peripheral vision. In tunnel vision you will most often have to move in a backward manner before angling side-ways to avoid the strike. (Figure 26) When using peripheral vision you will be able to move to a side angle with greater ease.

Now apply what you've learned about the leaning factor and combine it with the use of peripheral vision. Take a preparatory posture with your partner, leaning slightly to one side.

The lean is accomplished by lifting the heel on one side (keeping knee straight) to shift the body to the other side. Us-

Figure 27

Figure 28

Figure 29

ing peripheral vision mode, have your partner punch quickly at you. Your objective is to move (sideways) as soon as you detect motion. Your reaction time and ability to move should be quicker and easier. (Figures 27 & 28)

Peripheral vision also broadens the area of your visual plane, allowing you to detect motion in a much broader area. This is extremely helpful when dealing with multiple attackers, allowing you enhanced timing for evasion and interception of the attackers' motion. When dealing with multiple attackers, you cannot focus on any single attacker. (Figures 27-29)

In this chapter we've discussed quite a bit about peripheral vision and it's advantages in relation to martial arts and escaping. We must also realize that tunnel vision is equally important. When dealing with evasion and escaping, peripheral vision is superior, but in attack mode tunnel vision is extremely important for focus and direction of speed, power, and projection of your spirit. So when dealing with the attack, we use peripheral vision to enhance our escaping & repositioning skills until we have placed the attacker in a vulnerable position. We then switch to tunnel vision for the attack enabling us to deliver powerful, focused strikes.

Peripheral vs. Tunnel Attitude

As students of the martial arts and life, we must always look to translate the martial physical concepts into principles to enhance our daily lives. In this instance, we look at peripheral and tunnel vision, and translate vision into attitude. How can we use what we know about peripheral and tunnel vision to guide us in our daily lives?

When someone has a peripheral attitude towards what they are doing, they have a flow about them. Let's first relate this to a martial technique. You are attempting to perform a throwing technique on your opponent. As you apply the technique, you create an effect (off-balancing him/her) but do not get the desired result (throwing opponent to ground) you anticipated. With peripheral attitude, you will take the effect (off-balance) presented to you and flow into another course of action to finish the opponent.

This may mean changing the initial direction of the throw or flowing into a striking combination, ending with the defeat of your opponent. If you were to have a tunnel attitude towards the

technique you are applying, and do not get the anticipated result, you will probably try to force the technique into working. This usually results in frustration. Learn to take the effect you create and flow with it into another option. Don't allow your prejudices to dictate your course of action.

Is this any different than how we should deal with daily life? Wouldn't our lives be more fulfilling if we learned to flow with challenges in our lives? How much stress could you eliminate in your life by adapting the concept of Mizu No Kokoro (mind like water) into your life? Water is one of the most powerful forces in nature. Water doesn't care how it gets to its destination. It takes the path of least resistance and moves around blockages and challenges. Taking on a peripheral attitude can help us accomplish this.

However, having a tunnel attitude in life is also extremely important when the situation requires it. How often in our lives do we struggle to gain proper focus to achieve a goal or overcome a challenge? When it comes to a goal, we must concentrate our efforts into specific steps necessary to reach our objective. We must lay out a strategy and create a map to reach our desired destination. We must attack overcoming a challenge in much the same manner. When faced with a challenge or problem, we must focus on the solution instead of the problem.

Focusing on the solution directs our energies forward in a positive and concentrated manner. Focusing on the problem wastes energy and creates imbalance in our lives. So as you can see, having a tunnel attitude is equally important as having a peripheral attitude. The key is to recognize when and where to use each attitude to our greatest benefit. Having the ability to have a focused, concentrated effort towards what we wish to accomplish and the ability to be flexible and adaptable when roadblocks come our way, allows us to become masters of our own destiny.

Projection and Retraction

We must understand the projection and retraction of the body and how each one is reliant on the other. Realize that every time we project a part of our body, there is a retracting motion that also takes place. How can we use this information to enhance our martial ability?

In the basic manner of throwing punches from a chambered position, our focus is usually on the projecting part of the punch. For now though, let's concentrate on the retracting side. Let your retracting side start the motion and pull that arm back quickly using that same side hip and shoulder. You should notice quite a difference in the speed and power generated from this exercise. Realize that the projecting and retracting sides must work together.

Now try the same exercise, this time concentrating on starting the motion with the retracting side (pulling back quickly) and twisting and transferring the speed and power into the projecting side. You should be able to generate a greater amount of speed and power from this exercise, as well as understanding how the two sides of the body must work in unison with each other. There is a certain balance that must be applied for optimum results.

Let's look at the motion needed to project a front thrust kick (mae geri). In order for the lower body to project the leg forward, the upper body must lean back or retract slightly. The higher the kick, the more lean or retraction of the upper body is necessary. Try to kick without this counter balance and note the awkwardness and loss of power.

These are just a few examples of basic body motion that are governed by natural law. If we understand the laws that govern our bodies, we can start to look at how we can apply and use this against an opponent. For instance, in order for an attacker to throw a second punch (secondary rotation), he must retract the projected side and rotate the body to project the opposite side of the body, crossing his center to find you. Any manipulation of that retracting side will affect the projecting limb. Whether that manipulation is freezing or stopping the retracting side, speeding it up, or manipulating the arm up or down, it will have an effect on the intended path of the projecting side. Practice this slowly with a partner to gain an understanding of this concept.

When we look at the concept of projection and retraction, the thought of balance should come to mind. With this in mind, we must also look for the philosophical applications for daily life. In this sense, what we give to the universe (family, jobs, hobbies, community, giving/doing for others, etc.) would be projection. Retraction would be what we receive from our universe (time to rest, companionship, love, satisfaction for what we do, money, etc.) are equally important for balance in our lives. Understand that there must be a balance between the giving and taking we do in our lives. Too often we end up focusing and placing more importance on one or the other.

Technique Evolution-Large to Small

Evolution is something that usually takes place naturally in life. The general process of development of everything we do or create is usually "Large to Small." Think back, if you can, to the first computer system, cell phone, or an early automobile. Think about how big your letters were when you first started writing the alphabet. It seems this is a natural process of evolution. This concept applies to the evolution of a student's martial technique, but as importantly, his or her personal development. As beginners, it is much easier for us to see and imitate large motions. It is easier to see the physical workings of a martial concept in a large technique, than in that of a tight, concise or subtler technique.

Let's look at some basic martial techniques and compare the use of this concept.

Technique #1 – Basic avoidance & parry block

Defender starts with target manipulation by leaning to angle #4 (Figure 30).

Figure 30   **Figure 31**   **Figure 32**

Attacker strikes with a right punch, defender steps out to angle #3 to avoid the punch (Figure 31). After repositioning, the defender executes a left-right parry block (Figure 32).

Technique #1 – Using minimal motion escaping & blocking

In the following sequence, the defender is going to perform the same technique, only with much smaller and tighter motion. The defender starts with the same leaning motion in Figure 33. Then as the attacker strikes with a punch, the defender will shift his weight back to angle #3 and project his right hip and hands (forming a triangle) out to angle #5, escaping the path of the strike and placing hands outside punch (Figure 34). In Figure #35, the defender rotates his hips and adjoining triangle, which parries the strike.

Figure 33   Figure 34   Figure 35

Figure 36   Figure 37   Figure 38

Technique #2 Cross wrist grab with basic repositioning

In technique #2, the attacker grabs the defender's right wrist with his own right hand (Figure 36).

| **Figure 39** | **Figure 40** | **Figure 41** |

In an attempt to take on less mass or weaken the strength of the attacker's grab, the defender steps out to the left (angle #3) and traps the attacker's grabbing hand (Figure 37).

By repositioning to the outside of the attacker's right hip, the defender is able to circle the grabbed hand around to apply a basic lock to attacker's wrist (Figure 38).

Technique #2a Using minimal motion repositioning

The attacker performs a right cross wrist grab (Figure 39).

In this variation, instead of stepping outside of the area of attacker's center or strength, the defender rotates and projects his right hip to the outside of the attacker's right hip and traps the grabbing hand (Figure 40).

This repositioning pushes the defender's body and grabbed hand to the outside of the attacker's strength and to the outside of his grabbing arm, allowing ease in applying the basic wrist lock. (Figure 41).

It is a natural part of the learning process, to identify and imitate large movements. This gives us the basic foundation on which to build on. But realize that the larger the motion, the larger the voids in that motion. These voids are what your opponent wants to fill in order to intercept and counter your action, to defeat you.

Experiment with ways to tighten up your motion, whether it's a basic fundamental, a kata, or a specific self-defense technique. Remember to take into consideration the laws of balance, proper triangulation, and the use of 7/10 when projecting any type of strike or block (the concept of 7/10 will be discussed later in this chapter). These guidelines will help tighten up your motion, as well as eliminate voids for the attacker to fill.

It is important to refine our martial abilities, but equally or even more important is our refinement as a person. How can we accomplish this in terms of our personal development? Large to small can relate to our refinement of our mental focus, streamlining areas of our life that need

more organization, focusing attention on vital areas of importance in our life, conserving the amount of energy we use and directing that energy in areas of importance.

What areas of your life could you better direct and focus your energies on? Maybe your professional life, your personal relationships, or certain life goals or dreams you may have?

Contour Striking/Crease Striking

The strategic use of striking to manipulate the body into each of your strikes is known as Contour Striking. When using this concept, the student must be aware of how the body reacts to being struck, how striking the creases of the body causes folds and brings the body into incoming strikes. Let's look at how the body naturally responds to a strike.

In Figure 42 through 44, you'll see some of the different effects caused by certain strikes.

In Figure 42, the attacker is arched backward from a strike to the face. In Figure 43, the attacker is folded forward by striking the waist crease.

The last photo (Figure 44) shows striking the arm downward to bring the head in to be struck.

| Figure 42 | Figure 43 | Figure 44 |

Learning how to use and target your strikes to cause different effects on your opponent's body is essential. Experimenting with a training partner to learn what strike causes what effect is of the utmost importance. Study the creases and how to manipulate them by striking to set up your attacker for follow-up strikes. In the next couple of pages we will show some examples of Contour Striking or Crease Striking.

Figure 45   Figure 46   Figure 47

Figure 48   Figure 49   Figure 50

In this sequence of photos, the attacker throws a right punch to the head, and the defender steps/ escapes out to angle #3 and aligns mid-level triangles (Figure 45). In Figure 46, the attacker rotates to throw a left punch, but the defender attacks the waist crease with a right front thrust kick to bring the attacker's head into range of a hand strike. The defender then slides in and strikes with double-crossing palm strikes (Figure 47). The defender then flows from double palms into a right elbow strike (Figure 48), right back fist (Figure 49), left palm heel strike, which arches the attacker back (Figure 50).

Figure 51

Figure 52

Figure 53

In the next example, the attacker throws a right punch and the defender slips inside to angle #4, and aligns triangles (Figure 51).

On the rotation of the attacker's second punch, the defender offsets the attacker's balance by striking to the face with the left hand (Figure 52).

The defender then strikes the waist crease in a downward angle, to fold the body forward, bringing the head into striking range (Figure 53).

This allows the defender to finish with an elbow strike to the head (Figure 54).

Manipulation of your attacker's creases contributes to the destruction of his balance and structure. As we destroy structure, we take away the attacker's ability to strike freely, with speed and power.

Figure 54

Striking and manipulating creases is also a powerful tool to be used in the practice of your throwing arts. As an individual grabs you he structures his footwork and body around that grab. In the following example, the attacker grabs the left lapel of the defender (Figure 55). The defender then strikes the elbow crease, directing it down and in towards the center line

(Figure 56), then front thrust kicks to crease the knee (Figure 57). This strike removes the attacker's ability to strike with the free hand, as well as destroys all structure and balance. (Note: You must keep the elbow creased, keeping the body folded.)

The defender then strikes upward into the face with a palm heel. This creases the neck and arches the spine (Figure 57). The defender maintains the arch of the attacker's spine, and moves his center into the attacker, throwing him to a backward angle (Figure 58).

Figure 55

Figure 56

Figure 57

Figure 58

Figure 59

Triangulation

Triangulation is a very important concept that will be used in almost every aspect of your martial arts, from your blocking, striking, throwing, and joint locking. When we are discussing this concept, understand that there is YOUR triangulation that you need to be aware of, AND your attacker's triangulation. Let's look at both perspectives.

Your Triangulation

When we talk about your triangulation as a defender, we need to look at several triangles on the body. The easiest one to see would be one of your upper body triangles, which would be from shoulder to shoulder to point of contact with the hands (Figure 60). When we operate from this position, we move more easily, block and strike more effectively, and are able to execute throwing and locking techniques more efficiency.

Everything we do is stronger and more effective when done from center. Would you attempt pick up a heavy package without aligning your center with what you want to lift? No, you center yourself with the object naturally. You don't really have to think about it. Then why don't we perform our martial arts with that attitude? In my mind, it's because we fail to recognize the similarities between natural everyday motion and our martial arts movements. We need someone who has traveled the path before us to point out aspects that we cannot see at the time.

Below are three more examples of your personal triangulation. Figure 61 shows the triangle base starting from third eye to hara, and then extending to point of contact with the hands. Figure 62 shows the base from hip-to-hip, extending to point of contact with the hands. Figure 63 shows the base of the triangle being knee-to-knee or foot-to-foot, to the point of contact with the hands.

Figure 60

Figure 61

Figure 62

Figure 63

Look at the following examples of a blocking technique. Notice the different body mechanics and attitude of the technique. Ask yourself which posture and attitude you would rather have when engaging an opponent. Both techniques have application and validity, but consider which posture and attitude fit which specific situation. In our martial arts, as well as in life, we need to make sure that our action or responses properly fit the situation. To think otherwise is like taking a knife to a gunfight!

Figure 64	Figure 65	Figure 66
Figure 67	Figure 68	Figure 69

In the above photos, the defender steps out of the path of the punch and executes a middle block. Notice how the defender's center is facing off to the 45-degree angle, making it difficult to employ his weapons against further attack. On a secondary punch the easiest option is a total escape in this direction.

In the second set of photos, the defender steps out to angle #3, escaping the path of the punch, then executes a middle block and rotates his center toward the centerline of the attacker. Notice the triangles formed by the defender. The aligning of the back hip is essential to load the body for attacking the opponent. Could he perform effective and timely blocking, hand striking, or kicking from this position? Yes, his triangulation is proper for this. In the last photo, he engages with a hand combination.

Proper   **Improper**

Now start to look at your throwing, striking, and locking. How can you use triangulation to effectively enhance these other areas of your martial arts?

When applying a joint lock, be sure to align your triangles to the joint that you are locking. Keeping your center lined up with the opponent allows for better weight transfer and weight settling into the lock. It is very easy to allow your center to drift away and disconnect with your hands during transitions in a locking technique. If this connection is disrupted, the strength and integrity of the lock will be compromised and will allow the opponent to counter it. Remember that keeping the elbows in close to the body allows for tighter, more effective triangles.

Back   **Front**

Opponent's Triangulation

In thinking about your opponent's triangulation and how to best manipulate body structure and balance, we must look at the attacker's base.

If you are attempting a throwing technique on your attacker, look at the position of his/her feet. Using the feet as the base of the triangle, find the point of the triangle in front and to the back of the attacker. These are the two directions in which it is easiest to put your opponent off-balance. Think of yourself sitting on a three-legged stool. If suddenly one of the legs were to break, your body would fall in that direction.

This is a very simple concept for even the beginner student to grasp, but extremely important for learning to recognize how to create loss of balance. Manipulating the attacker's body structure in these directions will result in limited balance and stability.

The concept of triangulation is an extremely important principle to understand. Use of this concept provides options, which in a self-defense situation is invaluable. Experiment with a training partner employing triangulation in your blocking, throwing, striking, and locking. See the possibilities that were not readily seen before...enjoy the process!

Concepts of 7/10 & Move Twice

Any projected motion should be executed with the force of 7, the secondary motion done with the force of 10. The concept of 7/10 is vast. It is a concept that can be applied in all areas of escaping, throwing, locking, and striking.

Let's explore some examples of this concept. A basic example of this concept would be in the application of a punch. When we strike an opponent with a punch, our objective is to penetrate the target area and introduce destructive energy. If we strike and penetrate the opponent's body, and do not retract our motion immediately after impact, two things will happen. One would be that you allow your striking limb to be grabbed or struck. The second would be that energy projection from your strike would be ineffective due to the maintained connection between you and your opponent. If you strike an opponent and retract quickly after impact, your energy will enter. If instead, we maintain contact after impact, the energy will reverse back into the striking limb. Thus, the retracting motion should be done faster than the projected motion.

Another example of this concept would be implemented in your escaping. In this instance, the attacker is preparing to throw a right punch (Figure 70). The defender is already positioning himself by leaning toward angle #4. The attacker throws the right punch, and the defender slips out to angle #3 (Figure 71). The attacker immediately throws the left punch, and the defender slips back to angle #6. The second escape is done faster than the first; due to the fact the attacker is following the momentum of his first punch (Figure 72).

Let's look at another example of how to use 7/10, and introduce the complementary concept of Move Twice in an application of joint locking. Sometimes when we apply a joint lock, the defender may reposition a leg to regain stability, in order to resist the lock. To try to continue

| Figure 70 | Figure 71 | Figure 72 |

applying the lock in the same direction can be difficult since the attacker's base has readjusted. In Figure 73 the defender is attempting to apply an outer wristlock. As the attacker feels the loss of balance, he moves his right foot out to stabilize. The defender, feeling the resistance to the lock, rotates the lock towards his right, causing the attacker to adjust once again (Figure 74).

The defender immediately rotates back to the left to reapply the lock (Figure 75). This second rotation is done faster than the first to keep the attacker off balance.

| Figure 73 | Figure 74 | Figure 75 |

As with the above example, the Move Twice Concept teaches a student how to deal with resistance when applying a technique. The student must first understand the concept, and how it applies to the technique. Then, the student must develop a feel for the attacker's resistance, and how to properly apply it.

Let's take the following example. The attacker throws a right punch, and the defender slips inside punch to angle #4 (Figure 76). The defender guides the punching arm down and in, creating a fold on the attacker (Figure 77). Immediately following the fold, the defender strikes the attacker's face, with a forearm strike to arch the spine (Figure 78). The defender then rotates the left leg behind, pivoting the hips and upper body, to complete the throw. As the attacker feels his loss of balance, he repositions his right leg for support, allowing himself the ability to resist the throw (Figure 79). The defender, feeling the resistance, immediately reverses the direction of the throw towards the back triangulation point to finish the throw (Figure 80).

Figure 76

Figure 77

Figure 78

Figure 79

Figure 80

Resistance–Adjustment–Redirection

Life doesn't always go as planned...in fact it rarely does!

Whether you're talking about the execution of a martial arts technique or simply plans made in daily life, complications arise, variables change.

The ability to adapt to changing environmental circumstances or factors is one of the most important aspects of survival. When we feel resistance in our personal lives, professional lives, or in our martial arts, we need to recognize it for what it is...conflict.

First we must identify the conflict. Then, we must analyze it.

Is this conflict worth acknowledging?

Must it be addressed?

If it must be addressed, what are our options?

Is compromise an option?

If so, we must negotiate and move on towards our intended goal.

If not, what action must we take to accomplish our intended objective?

The Concept of Resistance–Adjustment

Figure 81

Figure 82

Figure 83

Figure 84

Figure 85

Redirection is merely another way of dealing with what comes your way, with a peripheral attitude. In the martial sense, when an attacker is providing resistance or has countered our intended technique, we must have the skills and the options to end the conflict.

In the following example of this, the attacker has grabbed the defender in a choke (Figure 81).

The defender attempts to apply an outward wristlock to throw the opponent (Figure 82).

As the defender applies the lock, the attacker readjusts his footwork to regain balance and provides resistance against the attempted lock (Figure 83).

The defender, feeling the resistance, uses the existing folds of the body and strikes upward to arch the head and spine back toward the attacker's triangle point (Figure 84).

The defender stays connected with the strike, stepping into the attacker, applying a throw to the back angle (Figure 85).

Elbow Awareness

Awareness of the positioning of our elbows has a dynamic impact on the effectiveness of our martial arts technique. How we position and apply our elbows in the process of a martial arts technique, or in an everyday task, can make all the difference when it comes to a balanced, efficient motion. The concept of Elbow Awareness, is yet another factor which is essential to understanding balance, and as importantly, to understanding how to negatively affect someone else's balance.

Notice how keeping the elbows in close to our bodies when performing common tasks, allows for a more stable, balanced motion. Notice how, when reaching for something, we naturally keep the elbow positioned downward towards the ground. Understand that any rotation of the extended arm, which rotates the elbow joint outward or inward, directs the body's balance in that direction.

Try this exercise…

Reach for a glass of water, or small object that is just out of reach, in front of you. Notice that as you extend your arm and elbow, once you pass a certain point, your body starts to lose balance in that direction, due to the body's natural folding to eliminate the distance between you and the object. Now, recreate the same reaching motion, only this time, experiment by rotating the elbow in an outward and inward direction. Notice how manipulating the direction of the elbow shifts the balance of the body in that direction.

Understand also that there is a direct relationship between the elbow and the knee. For instance, notice how when the elbow is creased, from a grab situation, the knees tend to crease or bend also. When we tense or lock our elbows, we eliminate the mobility of our knees. With this in mind, the awareness of how we posture our own elbows promotes better balance and structure.

Taking this information, now we must study how manipulation of an opponent's elbow, can offset his balance and structure. Notice how manipulating an opponent's elbow in different directions, rolls the weight to various parts of the feet. If we direct or manipulate the elbow in towards the opponent's center, the weight and balance point shifts back onto the heels.

Take a moment and experiment with this. Stand in a natural posture and throw a punch at an imaginary opponent. As you retract the arm, draw the elbow back into your center and touch your chest. You should feel the balance point shifted back onto your heels. Feel how difficult it is to throw a powerful, effective second punch from this position.

Now, repeat the same exercise, this time on retraction of the arm, suddenly push the elbow outward, as if an opponent was manipulating it. This motion shifts the balance point to the balls of the feet. Again, as the weight shifts to the balls of the feet, try to throw a powerful, effective punch. Now take time with a training partner to experiment with elbow manipulation. Throw a punch at your partner, having him slip to the outside of the strike, and contact the elbow area of the extended punch. As you retract slowly, have your partner control the elbow and direct it back into your center, shifting your weight back onto your heels.

Then perform the same exercise, this time after slipping to the outside of the punch, have your partner contact the elbow, guiding it slightly outward and downward, shifting your weight and balance to the balls of the feet. Make sure your partner is using their hips to guide the motion of your arm/elbow.

Take your time and experiment with manipulating the elbow to all angles of the octagon. Feel how directing the elbow to different angles shifts body weight and balance to different areas of the feet.

Please note that these manipulations must be done on a moving, weightless partner. Not on a structured, stationary partner.

Having an awareness of elbow manipulation, and how it effects freezing and creasing of the knees, is a very important tool for your throwing, striking, and locking arts as well. Execute your various throws and locks, paying special attention to how directing the elbow in different directions creates different effects on your opponent's body. Notice how, when applying an outward wristlock or kotegaeshi, driving the elbow downward towards the center pole of the octagon, drops and brings the head in close for application of the striking arts. Experiment and observe!

Experiment with a training partner, having him attack with various grabs. Work on creasing the elbow and directing it to various angles of the octagon. Notice the different effects this has on your partner's balance and structure. Look at the variations for different throwing techniques that become available to you. Take your time...and observe.

Loading/Preparatory Motion

The preparatory action or motion needed to initiate movement from one stance or posture to the next is called loading. After settling into a structured, stance or posture, there must be a coiling motion to repel the body from this settled position. We as human beings are constantly fighting to overcome gravity. Every time we move from one posture to another, we have to overcome gravity to initiate our next motion. The concept of Loading or Preparatory Motion is about recognizing this factor, and looking deeply into this matter to observe how we may manipulate our structure, to allow for quicker, more direct movement.

How do we study this? The first thing we must do is slow down. Our body knows how to adjust for easier, more efficient motion. We need to pay attention to how the body adjusts and coils, to create new motion. Stand with your left foot forward, in a natural posture. Slowly, shift your body weight to take a step. Notice how certain muscle groups energize, or tense up, to initiate this motion. If the practitioner were to energize these muscle groups ahead of time, would they not be able to move in a more direct and efficient manner?

Pay attention to how the feet adjust when we decide to change the direction in which we move. Understand, that by adjusting our feet in order to turn to a specific direction, we also adjust our hip to help direct our body.

Observe how people walk. Notice how when moving forward, our bodies also move in a lateral (side-to-side) motion, shifting weight to one leg, in order to take a step forward with the other leg. This lateral motion takes time and energy, while also exciting the periphery of the opponent. In order to eliminate this lateral motion, the practitioner must adjust the heel of the foot under his body so that it is closer to his centerline.

In the next sequence of photos, the practitioner starts in a back stance (Figure 86), but adjusts the front heel inward towards his centerline, as a preparatory motion (Figure 87). This motion generally would be undetected by the opponent, being below his visual plane. With this reposition of the foot, not only is there less lateral motion on the transition, but also the left hip has been opened up for a smooth transition forward. This preparatory motion allows for a direct, uninhibited movement forward into striking range of the opponent. (Figure 88)

How can we experiment and practice this? Well, we can observe everyday motion.

Notice how the body adjusts to changes in direction. The practice of kata, is a perfect vehicle for understanding the use of preparatory motion, for quicker, more direct motion. In order to see or feel this, one must slow down. Realize the most important part of kata, is not the ending of each motion, but the initial part or transition of each motion. Observe, practice, and most of all, feel.

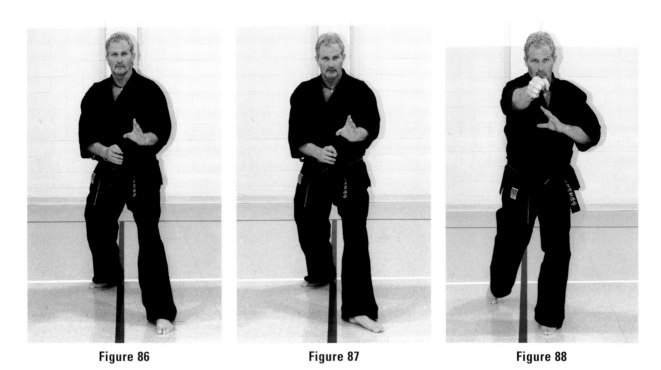

Figure 86   **Figure 87**   **Figure 88**

In this chapter, I hope to have given the reader examples and insights into concepts and principles that will enhance whatever martial art you may practice. It is my hope that this text will induce thought, and open doors to a deeper understanding of the martial arts and ourselves.

CHAPTER 7

Escaping

Escaping Arts

According to Mitose Sensei, "True self defense involves no body contact." Therefore the escaping arts are to be considered the highest level of the art. There are several reasons why this is so.

First of all, the concept of doing no harm to another individual, and allowing no harm to be done to yourself is the safest and most efficient form of self protection. With the use of the octagon and proper visual skills, the practitioner can detect motion and remove themselves from harm's way. The practitioner must study and understand the concepts of hyoshi (timing) and maai (distancing). The use of proper visual skills such as peripheral and tunnel vision must be understood and applied to everything we do.

Secondly, the use of proper escaping skills allows the practitioner to reposition his/her self to an area where the attacker must readjust his body to continue or follow through with the attack. This adjustment will take time, and will require the attacker to reposition and rotate this body to continue the attack. During this rotation, the attacker must readjust and cross his current centerline, therefore putting himself in a weightless state during the transition.

For instance, in Figure 89 the defender leans slightly to his right (angle #4) to give his attacker a false center to attack. The attacker then throws a right punch, and the defender slips out to his left (angle #3), and aligns triangles to the attacker's center. Note how the attacker must readjust his entire body and cross his centerline. (Figure 90)

As the attacker rotates to cross his centerline, he becomes weightless (Figure 91). At this point the attacker is vulnerable to body manipulations which disrupt balance and stability allowing the practitioner the ability to apply a nagae or throwing technique (Figure 92).

Also during this transition, as the attacker becomes weightless, his ability to absorb or withstand an atemi or striking technique, is considerably reduced (Figure 93).

With the use of the octagon, and proper distancing and timing, good escaping skills will allow the practitioner to disappear from the attacker's visual plane. This not only has a physical effect on your opponent, but also affects them mentally. This creates a state of confusion to place your opponent off balance mentally, as well as physically.

Figure 89   Figure 90   Figure 91

Figure 92   Figure 93

As discussed in other chapters, we have two basic options or attitudes when it comes to our escaping arts. The practitioner can either take on the attitude of total escape, or he may choose to escape and engage. Both attitudes are extremely useful, depending on the situation. Note the following pages illustrating these two approaches.

Octagon for Total Escape

Octagon for Escape and Engagement

Attitude of Total Escape

When we look at the mind-set of total escape, Mitose Sensei's words must come to mind, "The inner-most and true spirit of Kempo lies in humility and self-restraint." When we look at the mind-set of total escape, we have nothing to prove, and nothing to gain by doing harm to another individual. This type of self-defense, exemplifies humility and self-restraint.

When dealing with a total escape mind-set, the idea is to confuse and place the attacker off balance. This confusion results from the fact that you are never where your attacker thinks you'll be. The attacker's anger is what drives him to throw the first attack. The emotion of anger is easily turned into frustration when the attacker's needs are not met.

The mind-set of total escape is not hindered by attachment. Like the characteristics of water, it doesn't care how it gets to its destination...it just gets there. In total escape mode, the practitioner is peripheral to his environment. In the visual sense, the practitioner sees everything in his environment, but does not acknowledge any of it as important or credible. The defender merely moves when the time is right, avoiding any conflict that may arise. Mentally and emotionally, the practitioner is detached somewhat, so as not to be unbalanced by anything that happens. The mind is "not stuck," but free to move itself and the body as needed.

The Attitude of Escape & Engagement

Looking at the attitude of escape and engagement, we see that the initial escaping portion is much the same as that of total escape. The practitioner remains peripheral, seeing everything, but attached to nothing.

Escaping allows the defender to reposition himself to gain superior position on his opponent, so as to neutralize the threat. When the defending practitioner then decides to engage, he or she becomes focused on taking on the opponent. This focus may be to control the opponent through the use of a controlling type maneuver, such as a throw or joint manipulation. At this point of engagement, the practitioner can also utilize the destructive arts, such as striking, to terminate the confrontation.

As the practitioner focuses on engagement and finishing the confrontation, he or she does so with a peripheral attitude toward whatever technique is being applied. This allows the practitioner the ability to adjust, or change the technique, if he or she encounters problems.

The study of the escaping arts is vast, and extremely important. Proper escaping lays down the groundwork for proficiency in your throwing, locking, and striking arts. This is possible through escaping the opponent's mass, and gaining superior positioning.

Experiment with the angles of the octagon, with various modes of vision, and distances. Be aware of the amount of space you need to function, and operate with maximum efficiency. Then translate this understanding to how your opponent moves, and the space needed for him to start and continue an effective attack. Learn to use the angles to sacrifice space when needed, and use these same angles to intercept and rob your attacker of the space he needs to operate.

CHAPTER 8

Blocking

Kosho Ryu Blocking Uke Waza

There are so many different ways to perceive the art of blocking. We can think of blocking as merely derailing a strike away from its intended target. Or it could be perceived as striking an attacker's limb as it approaches you, destroying the arm, creating imbalance in their body. When we look at the term "uke," or to receive, we can see blocking as a way to safely receive someone's attack. When receiving, we must receive and create imbalance! Every opponent has a process of movement they must go through, repelling from their stationary posture to initiate the attack, through the weightless state of initial projection and extension of the strike, to the settling back into a form of stance. Therefore our blocking must have an off balancing effect on our opponent that makes this process difficult for them to execute quickly and efficiently. If that process is difficult, our job to manipulate them physically and mentally becomes easier, therefore allowing us to neutralize our opponent. There are many ways to look at blocking and more importantly, the attitude you put into a block. We will explore them in this chapter, hoping to enhance your insights into your blocking.

Always remember: Off Balance ➔ Manipulate ➔ Take Advantage!

Let's look at the different attitudes we should be aware of when executing blocking techniques. In the beginning of our training, we are concentrating on performing the block correctly and keeping ourselves from being struck. As we feel more confident and natural with our blocking techniques, we can start to apply the use of angles to make our blocking more effective. An extremely important element in our blocking has to be proper escaping! Repositioning ourselves to an angle where we do not take on the mass of the attacker and allows for ease in execution of the block. This also allows us to see many different applications for their use, as well as placing us in a superior position when dealing with a secondary strike. This is where the octagon becomes so incredibly important. The Octagon acts as a roadmap for proper positioning when dealing with an attacker.

When we attempt to block while staying in our opponent's line of attack, we will be forced to take on their body mass; also, if we move backward to receive their attack, we allow the opponent to continue their momentum towards us. The opponent has no need to readjust their center, to change the direction of the attack.

Notice that by moving backward to receive the strike, the attacker easily readjusts to throw a follow-up strike. The attacker never loses visual contact with the defender, and is not forced to readjust his center to throw a follow-up strike.

We know that two objects cannot occupy the same space at the same time. When an attacker strikes, he wants to occupy the space that we take up. The practitioner merely needs to give up that space, and occupy new space. The octagon angles allow us to move to an unoccupied space, giving us superior positioning over our opponent. That positioning may be to escape harm totally, or to use a controlling type technique, or to engage and finish the opponent.

In the above sequence of photos, the attacker throws a right punch, the defender slips out to angle #3 and blocks with a middle block (note the angle of attacker's center), as attacker rotates center, the defender throws a left punch to the face, as attacker is in transition. The key to this application is to angle out and escape, execute the middle block and align the triangle towards attacker's center. This alignment allows the defender to respond immediately, while the attacker must readjust and rotate to continue his attack.

When we execute a block, we need to have in mind, whether we choose to block and escape, or block and engage the attacker. This mindset determines how we align our center. This is dependent on what we choose to accept. The practitioner can choose to use the block to redirect the attack, and align him or herself to an angle for immediate escape; or redirect the attack and align center towards the attacker for engagement.

On the other hand, if the defender chooses to accept the attacker, and wishes to engage, he must escape to the angle and execute a block while aligning his center towards the attacker. This puts the defender in a position to immediately engage and strike the attacker. Practice executing your different basic blocks as you escape to the different angles of the octagon. Work an escape to each angle, and experiment with the mindset of blocking the incoming attack, and align center for total escape. Then, repeat the exercise with the mindset of immediately engaging the attacker, by aligning your center towards them.

| Figure 94 | Figure 95 | Figure 96 |

In the above photos, the attacker throws a right punch. The defender slips out to angle #3 (Figure 94) and executes a right middle block (Figure 95), with his center aligned towards angle #5. From this position, the defender's best option is total escape to angle #5 (Figure 96)

Notice how, when using the mindset of blocking and aligning center to engage, the options for throwing, striking, and locking become more available. Proper triangulation gives the practitioner full use of all his/her weapons, for use in eliminating structural balance of the opponent to accomplish a throwing (nagae) technique, or for the destruction of the opponent through the use of striking (atemi) techniques.

Keep in mind that use of your angles of escape, must be accompanied by the use of proper timing (hyoshi), and distancing (maai). The use of peripheral vision allows the practitioner to move on time, allowing for appropriate hyoshi. These points are discussed in more detail in the chapter on concepts.

On pages 117 and 118 you can find examples of blocking for use of escaping, and blocking to engage an opponent.

Look at the following sequences for examples of using the octagon for escaping and engaging the opponent, to execute throwing, striking, and locking techniques.

| **Figure 97** | **Figure 98** | **Figure 99** |

In Figure 97, the attacker throws a right punch, and the defender slips out to angle #3 and executes a kake uke or parry block. Note how the defender blocks and aligns center. In Figure 98, the attacker rotates to throw the left punch, and the defender slips inside the punch. As he escapes, he guides the left arm downward to create a fold, and strikes to the head with the left arm, to create an arch of the attacker's spine. With the attacker folded and arched, he steps behind and rotates (while keeping the attacker arched), thus creating a void for the attacker to fall into. (Figure 99) Note, if the defender's center was not aligned, he would not have enough time to adjust and execute the throw.

The next sequence of photos demonstrates the use of escape and alignment, for the use of implementing the striking arts. In Figure 100, the defender slips to angle #3, outside the right punch. He executes a parry block and aligns his triangles. As the attacker throws the left punch, the defender strikes with a punch to the projecting shoulder. This strike stops the incoming strike and freezes the attacker's structure. (Figure 101) The defender then immediately moves in to finish with a striking combination to the head. (Figure 102)

| **Figure 100** | **Figure 101** | **Figure 102** |

Blocking and aligning in this manner, allows the practitioner superior positioning (gamae). This posture and positioning, allows for quick direct striking, or for the use of manipulating the balance and structure of the rotating opponent.

The Attitude of Your Block

When performing anything in life, often the attitude you put into what you're performing makes all the difference! Different attitudes create different effects. Whether we're talking about life, or about the performance of your blocking technique, it's all the same. Your uke no waza or blocking technique, can take on several different attitudes. We can use the categories of hard and soft, or an attitude of striking, or yielding/manipulating.

If you were going to execute your block with a striking attitude, you would be taking on more of an offensive approach to blocking. The strike of your blocking motion may be to destroy a limb, or to attack a pressure point, rendering it temporarily useless.

The striking manner of your block may be used to strike the body or arm, to manipulate the spinal structure. Study the following photos for examples of these techniques.

In Figure 103, the attacker throws a right punch, and the defender slips out to angle #3. The defender uses the left cover hand of the block, to guide the punch out beyond his body, and then strikes the arm with the right block. (Figure 104) Refer to the chapter on Pressure Points for location of arm points to be struck.

In another example of the chudan uke, or middle block, the defender's wrist/ forearm has been grabbed. (Figure 105) The defender slides back to angle #2, to force the attacker's elbow joint to full extension, then the defender locks the joint by executing a chudan uke. (Figure 106)

Figure 103

Figure 104

Figure 105

Figure 106

In the above photos, the attacker steps in to throw a right punch. The defender moves in on the attacker's initial motion, contacting the attacker's arm at the center pole of the octagon, executing a jodan or high level block. This motion contacts the arm as the opponent's weight is rising and moving forward, which allows for ease in manipulating the opponent's spinal structure in a backward manner.

In the next series of photos, the attacker throws a punch, and the defender steps to the inside of the strike. The defender parries the blow with the right hand, and strikes the attacker's face with the rising portion of the block. Note that the escaping motion needed to slip the strike is of extreme importance.

The Essence of the Block

If we look at the essence of what we want our blocking technique to be about, we have to look at the various attitudes or approaches our blocks may take on.

Blocking that is yielding, and off-balancing
Blocking that is intercepting and redirecting, off-balancing
Blocking that is aggressive and striking in nature, off-balancing

Note the above approaches to blocking. All three of these approaches have a different essence, or attitude to the block. But all three are used to ultimately create imbalance.

Blocking just to stop a strike, if it does not create an off-balancing effect, is inefficient and wasteful. Our blocking maneuvers should not only safely keep us from being struck, but also have an unbalancing effect on our attacker. Once off-balanced, an attacker is easily manipulated for defeat! Therefore a block that takes away structure of an attacker, allows us the options of continuing with an effective throw, lock, or strike.

The Center Pole of the Octagon

If we look at blocking to or at the center pole of the octagon, our blocking takes on more of an intercepting motion. As discussed in other chapters, the area of the center pole is the neutral area that an opponent needs to occupy, in order to make contact with us. If we intercept our opponent's motion at this center pole area, our block will disrupt and manipulate the structure of our opponent. Understand that an attacker must repel from a stationary or settled position, in which the body weight must rise to move forward, and then settle into a stance to propel a strike. This rising motion creates a momentary weightless effect on them. A practitioner can use the octagon's center pole area in several ways.

The defender may move on the attacker's initial motion, taking up the center pole area with his body while projecting the block. Using proper hyoshi or timing, this option allows the defender to apply the blocking motion to an attacker whose weight is just starting to rise, intercepting their motion and disrupting balance and structure.

The second option for use of the center pole when blocking, would be to intercept the intended strike or grab at the center pole, making contact with the attacker's strike at approximately 1/2 extension of the projected strike. This intercepting motion jams and redirects the intended strike to an angle of safety, and causes an imbalance on the attacker by creating a fold of the body.

Explore the use of the center pole of the octagon, when applying your blocking techniques. Use it as a tool to intercept your attacker's motion. Vary the use of your targets areas on an opponent, as well as the timing of your blocks, when using the concept of the center pole of the octagon.

Blocks as Locks

As mentioned earlier, the use of your blocking motion can be used for striking an attacker. Also understand that these blocks can also be used to lock the joints of an attacker. Experiment and

Figure 107

Figure 108

Figure 109

study how the motion of a block can manipulate and lock joints of an attacker. These blocks/ locks can be used to totally destroy an attacker's joint to neutralize the situation, or used to destroy structure and balance for the use of finishing through throwing or striking techniques. Study the following examples on how to apply your blocking, for the use of kansetsu waza or locking techniques.

In the above sequence, the attacker throws a punch, and the defender slips out to angle #3 and parry blocks and grabs the wrist of the punching arm. (Figures 107 & 108) The defender retracts the right arm to hyper-extend the attacker's elbow, and uses a left inside forearm block to lock the elbow joint. (Figure 109)

In the next sequence, the attacker grabs the same side forearm of the defender. (Figure 110) The defender steps back with the left foot to off-balance hyper-extend the elbow, and brings the right arm up over the top of controlled arm. (Figure 111) The defender strikes with a downward block as the left arm retracts to lock the attacker's elbow. (Figure 112)

Note that the retracting hand/arm is essential to the locking process. This arm retracting quickly easily straightens and extends the elbow for the lock to be applied.

| Figure 110 | Figure 111 | Figure 112 |

| Figure 113 | Figure 114 | Figure 115 |

In the next sequence, the attacker grabs the left arm with his right hand. (Figure 113) The defender shifts back into a neko ashi dachi, or cat stance. This shifting of the weight backwards draws the elbow into the extended position. (Figure 114) The defender then executes an outside middle block to lock the elbow. (Figure 115)

Study the movement and motion of your various blocking techniques. Be aware not only of the projected motion, but just as important, the retracting motion. Experiment with the use of your various blocks, using proper escaping and alignment. Study how the motion of your blocks can translate in strikes, locks, and throws.

Blocking for Total Escape

Blocking and Realigning for Engagement

CHAPTER 9

Joint Locking

Kansetsu Waza (Joint Locking)

The locks and joint manipulation of Kosho Ryu Kempo, are similar to that of other arts. These locks/manipulations fall into the category of the controlling arts. These waza or techniques are meant for the use in controlling an opponent's aggression through the use of pain to gain compliance, and the off-balancing effects of locking of the skeletal structure. Remember balance and imbalance! Remember that kansetsu waza is about manipulating the skeletal structure to create imbalance within our opponent, while we maintain our own balance. Take the time to experiment with various skeletal manipulations, and the various off-balancing effects they produce on an opponent. Be aware of the opponent's balance points and their foundation. Notice the various creases they create...and how to manipulate those creases. Let's look at some basic locks, and study the effects they create.

Outward Wrist Lock - Kotegaeshi

Figure 116 **Figure 117** **Figure 118**

In Figure 116, the defender controls the attacker's hand. In Figure 117 the defender jams the elbow in a downward motion, locking the wrist. Notice the creases in the knees and at the waist. The defender then rotates around his center, turning the locked hand in an outward manner (Figure 118). Note the folding and creasing effects on the body. Notice how the attacker's head is out beyond the structure of his feet. With continued rotation by the defender, and the removal of a balance point (the defender's left leg), the attacker falls into the void. An important mind-set of the Kosho Ryu practitioner, when it comes to technical application, is a peripheral attitude—that is we are not locked in to a single threaded focus. Sometimes we don't get the

Figure 119 **Figure 120** **Figure 121**

intended result when we apply a joint lock. But we usually see some sort of effect from it. The practitioner, who maintains a peripheral mind-set, will take the effect created by the lock and use it to defeat an opponent.

For instance, let's take the joint lock we just covered. As the defender applies the outward wristlock (Figure 119), the attacker steps out with his right foot to catch his balance (Figure 120). Instead of trying to force the lock, the defender immediately takes the fold that was created, and manipulates the opponent's head to arch him toward his back triangulation point, applying a throwing technique (Figure 121).

Figure 122   **Figure 123**

In another example of this mind-set, the defender applies the outward wristlock. As the defender locks the joint and creases the elbow downward, the opponent's knees buckle and the upper torso is slightly folded (Figure 122). The defender feels some resistance, and immediately flows into a striking combination (Figure 123).

Take all your basic joint locks and experiment with the effects they create. Observe what effects take place on your training partner's body. Notice your options for attacking the body in these weakened states, through the use of your striking, throwing, kicking, or other joint manipulations.

Realize that if the attacker restructures his base during the application of the lock, you will feel resistance in the opposite direction of your application.

By using the concept of "Move Twice," you merely need to change the direction of force with the locked hand, and then immediately reverse the lock back in the intended direction. Realize that the body can only resist in one direction at a time. Therefore in this instance you move with the attacker's resistance, and immediately reverse it. Be extremely careful when executing this application, since this can seriously injure your training partner's joint.

In the next example, the attacker has grabbed the defender in a double choke position (Figure 124). The defender grabs the attacker's right hand and checks his elbow with his left hand. Since the attacker is in a balanced, structured posture, the defender kicks the shin of the attacker to

Figure 124

Figure 125

Figure 126

Figure 127

Figure 128

mentally off-balance him (Figure 125). The defender twists out of the choke, locking the wrist and elbow, causing the attacker to be folded at the waist (Figure 126). As the defender applies the locks, he feels the resistance of the attacker pushing upward (Figure 127). Feeling the resistance, the defender allows the attacker to rise, meeting his motion with an upward elbow strike to arch the body backward, into a throw. (Figure 128)

Remember that when attempting to apply a lock on a person who is in a balanced, structured position, the defender must divert the attacker's mental and physical focus to initiate the locking motion.

Another very important ingredient in successful joint locking is the ability to align your triangles with the joint you are manipulating. This, along with keeping the elbows in close to your body, allows for a connected, stable, and powerful application. Refer to the Concepts of Study chapter for more on triangulation.

Countering Joint Locks

As has been mentioned before in other chapters, the body needs a certain amount of space to operate. Apply a joint lock on a partner, and observe how much space is needed to be effective. When countering another person's joint lock, we need to understand how to manipulate that space, in order to make the lock ineffective. An effective way of doing this would be to move your center in towards the lock. This reinforces the defender's strength and stability, while jam-

ming the attacker, by taking up their operational space. Refer to the chapter on the octagon, and manipulation of the center pole. View the following photos for an example of this.

Another important factor to remember when countering joint locks is the manipulation of the attacker's elbows. Controlling the motion of the attacker's elbows inhibits their free range of motion, making their application difficult.

Experiment with a training partner on this. Have your partner slowly apply a lock. Observe how the elbows move. Then work on freezing one of your partner's elbows, inhibiting its ability to move properly. Observe how this creates difficulty for your partner's application. Then repeat this process, this time by manipulating the intended path of motion the elbow takes. Note how manipulating this path, causes over-movement by your partner. Notice any folds or creases this may create, and how you may take advantage of them, to disable your partner from further action.

Kata Bunkai for Joint Locking

Most martial art systems practice kata as part of their training programs. But many times, the application is not taught except for the obvious blocks, punches, and kicks. The word bunkai, can be translated into the exploration encouraging a deeper look into your studies.

Remember that the performance of a block in your kata should be able to be translated into a strike, a throw, or a joint lock. Look at any blocking motion in your kata. Observe the retracting arm and side of the body. Notice how this retracting arm, could be used to hyperextend the projecting arm of your opponent into a joint lock.

In the first sequence of photos, the defender's right forearm is grabbed by the attacker's right hand. The defender rolls the grabbed hand around and onto the attacker's forearm to grab it. The defender shifts back to angle #2, drawing the attacker off-balance, and extending the arm so the elbow is straight. The defender then contacts the elbow joint with a forearm block to lock the elbow. Once the lock is applied, the defender takes the attacker to the ground.

In much the same manner, the next sequence of photos shows the attacker grabbing the same side arm. The defender again rolls the hand around, to grab and secure the attacker's arm. Then shifting back to hyper-extend the elbow joint. The defender then executes an outward middle block to lock the elbow joint.

In the final sequence of photos, the defender applies locks to the attacker using the motion of a low block.

The art of joint manipulation is vast. There is so much to study and observe. I hope the material in this chapter opens the doors to new ideas of study and application for the reader. Practice your locks, observe the effects, and understand how to manipulate the balance and structure of your opponent.

CHAPTER 10

Throwing

Nagae - Throwing Arts

When I first saw the throwing arts of Kosho Ryu, I was amazed at how effortless it seemed for Hanshi Bruce Juchnik to accomplish each technique. My martial arts background at that point had included little or no throwing experience. I remember there were no gaps or pauses in his defenses and he could accomplish a throw from just about any position in relation to his opponent. Most of the throwing I had seen prior to that had seemed to require a great deal of strength, leverage, and a very specific body type.

When I decided to study Kosho, I thought that this would be a very difficult area for me to excel in, due to my lack of experience. When I began to study with Hanshi, I expected to be taught a variety of different techniques to enhance my throwing abilities. Instead, I was exposed to studying balance and how to manipulate it. I was confused and a bit impatient. Hanshi would say *"If you want to learn to throw, throw yourself."* This type of learning was very different for me. I was used to being taught a specific technique to be done in a specific manner. Yet as time passed, I realized what I was experiencing was far more important than learning a series of prearranged throwing techniques. I was learning the principles and concepts that make all throws work. Let's look at some of the important components that contribute to the effectiveness of the throwing arts.

Escaping was considered the highest art by Professor James Mitose, the 21st generation Headmaster of Kosho Ryu Kempo. Proper positioning is extremely important in any type of confrontation, whether it be physical or verbal. One of the most important aspects of throwing is the ability to escape and reposition yourself to make your attacker reposition himself and cross his center. It is this repositioning movement that weakens your attacker and makes him vulnerable to your manipulation.

Let's discuss some of the key points to manipulating balance and creating throwing techniques.

1) The 4 directional folds

The 4 directional folds of the body take place at the center or waist crease. The body can be folded towards angle #1 (forward), to angle #2 (backward), to angle #3 (left side), and to angle

#4 (right side) (Figures 128-31). The key to balance is keeping your spine structured so that your weight is directly over your feet.

So, to destroy balance we want to manipulate the skeletal structure so the head is out beyond the support of the feet. The four directional folding drill is used to experiment with this concept.

Angle 1

Angle 2

Angle 3

Angle 4

2) Creasing of the body

Proper knowledge of how to use the natural creases of the body in conjunction with the four major folds is extremely important. This knowledge allows you to create an unlimited number of throws from any type of situation.

Manipulating the creases of the body, such as the elbow in a grab situation, gives the defender easy access along with the ability to affect the spine into the four directional folds. Take the time to work with a training partner and experiment with all the creases to see how easy it is to create imbalance in the body. Look for creases at the wrists, elbows, shoulders, neck, waist, hips, knees, and ankles.

Also, experiment to see how these creases can be used in conjunction with each other. This allows for multiple options in the event a technique creates an effect, but doesn't give you the

Wrist crease

Using the effect of the wrist crease to arch spine and apply throw

Elbow crease

Arch spine & apply throw

anticipated result. Study the following photos on creasing and notice how they contribute to the destruction of the opponent's balance and allow for multiple options for throwing techniques.

In the below sequence, the defender attacks the elbow crease and the knee crease to break down the structure of the attacker, then arches his back/spine to create the throw.

Crease elbow   **Crease knee with kick**   **Arch spine & throw**

In the next sequence, we attack the elbow crease first, then immediately attack the waist crease bringing the head in, arching the spine.

When you are working on manipulating the elbow crease in grabbing situations, experiment with creasing it from the inside of the grabbing arm as well as from the outside. Look for different effects this has on the structure of the spine and what different options you have for throws. Then, work on creasing the elbow from the inside and outside, but this time manipulate towards different angles of the octagon. Look at the effects and the options for your throwing techniques. Study the following photos for different examples of creasing the elbow to different angles.

Crease elbow   **Crease waist**   **Arch spine and rotate**

When creasing the elbow, you must be aware of the opponent's foundation for support. Notice when creasing the elbow downward, the opponent will try to restructure their support by shifting one of their feet to a position under the point where the elbow is being directed. This is done naturally to save their balance.

By being aware of this, creasing downward and to a side angle, you eliminate your opponent's ability to restructure his foundation. This relates to the concept of your opponent's triangulation, which will be covered later in this chapter.

3) Creating the void

When we think of a void, we think of some kind of space into which objects fall, filling the void. Knowledge of how to create and use the void when it comes to throwing can make the difference between having to force a throw or being able to accomplish the technique with minimal effort and economy of motion.

Figure 132   **Figure 133**   **Figure 134**

As we've said before, one loses balance when the spinal structure is manipulated so the weight is out beyond the foundation of the feet. At this point, creating a rotation on that structure makes it difficult for the opponent to recover balance. Also, realize that when off balancing an opponent in a throwing technique, your legs become a point of balance for your opponent. Removing a leg that is contributing to the balance of your opponent by rotating it behind your body, takes this balance point away to create a void for him to fall into. It is very important to make your opponent dependent on this balance point by folding his body in that direction (bringing his head out beyond his feet) so when you remove the leg he will fall into the void. Study Figures 132-134.

4) Where is your opponent's triangulation balance point?

Triangulation is a concept that has applications in all aspects of martial study, from blocking and striking, to throwing and the manipulation of balance. It is a concept that ties directly to creating the void, which we just covered. An opponent's triangulation balance point can be found by merely drawing a line from the opponent's left foot to their right foot. Then find the triangle point about three feet directly in front of them and directly behind them. These are the two directions in which opponent will be weakest in maintaining his balance.

Figure 135

Figure 136

This can be compared to the third leg of a stool. If the third leg were to break, the weight would shift to that direction and loss of balance would cause the stool to fall in that direction. When you are engaged with an opponent and are manipulating his structure and balance, you become his triangulation balance point (Figure 136).

So, as we discussed in the concept of creating the void, you must be able to remove this balance point to create a void for the opponent to fall into.

5) The arm is merely a lever to affect the spine

This concept is essential in understanding how to use the extending striking or grabbing arm to create imbalance in the opponent's spinal structure. When we redirect the extending arm, we create slight imbalance in the spinal structure. This sounds like an easy concept to grasp and use, but take your time and experiment with this.

Direct to Angle 4

Direct to Angle 6

Direct to Angle 1

Direct to Angle 5

When an opponent is attacking you, he would most likely be projecting an arm towards you in order to strike or grab you. Since the arm is moving towards you, it is closer and easier to manipulate than the torso of the body. Work with a training partner and have him project single punches and grabs at a slow to medium speed. Your objective is to manipulate the path of the strike or grab and observe the effect it has on the spinal structure. Place a mental octagon on your opponent and manipulate the path of the extending limb to the different angles and observe the different folds/creases and options that are available for throwing.

Once you've manipulated the intended path of the strike or grab and placed your opponent in a vulnerable position, continue to destroy your opponent's structure by attacking creases such as the neck, waist, and knees to throw your opponent.

Next, take the same exercise and have your training partner perform different grabs on you. Let the grab take place and manipulate the grabbing limb (elbow crease) to the different angles of the octagon, again observing the effects on your partner. Remember several key considerations when working this drill. First, start moving/manipulating the grabbing arm just as the grab takes place. Do not allow your partner to realign his body to control the motion of your arm. When an opponent extends his arm to grab, he will have to reach for you, creating a slight fold and imbalance in his body. This off balancing motion will momentarily prevent your opponent from controlling the grab. But, he will automatically compensate by restructuring his body so he'll be able to strengthen the grab. It is just before this restructuring takes place that we must manipulate the opponent's grabbing arm to different angles of the octagon.

Manipulate neck crease   **Manipulate waist crease**   **Manipulate knee crease**

When manipulating the grab, make sure to maintain your own triangulation. For instance, let's say your opponent has grabbed your wrist. Your triangle would be from hip-to-hip to the center point of the triangle, where your grabbed wrist should be. This would be the position where you would be centered and strongest in terms of being able to move the opponent's arm to create imbalance. If you allow your arm to leave this triangle, you will only have the strength of your arm as opposed to the strength of your entire body. Now as we direct the opponent's grabbing arm to different angles of the octagon, start to reposition your feet to take away the support or balance point of the opponent. After directing the opponent's grabbing arm to an angle and manipulating their structure, immediately attack creases such as the neck, waist,

| Figure 137 | Figure 138 | Figure 139 |

and knees to completely destroy the structure of the opponent for a throw. Note the following photos for examples.

Figure #137 shows the defender creasing his attacker's elbow down and inward to angle #6, then immediately creasing knee with a kick (Figure 138), and following up with a right strike to arch the head backward (Figure 139) and continue to throw.

6) Move Twice

Every action you take against an opponent has an equal and opposite reaction. The concept of Move Twice is so vast and applies to so many aspects of self-defense. For now, we will look at how we can use this for throwing purposes. Let's look at what happens when we direct or manipulate an opponent's balance. The opponent will naturally resist and try to readjust in an opposite direction in an attempt to regain structure and balance. When this action takes place, you must redirect your force in order to use the opponent's strength against him.

For example, if you and your opponent are pulling in two different directions, trying to pull each other off balance, and you suddenly change the direction of your force and begin to push instead of pulling, your opponent will fall backwards. You will be using your opponent's force against him. This concept is a very powerful tool to have in your arsenal.

Your opponent can only resist in one direction at a time. Think of how many times you've been working a throwing technique only to have the opponent catch their balance half way through and resist in the opposite direction of your technique. Generally, the first reaction is to resist your opponent's strength and try to force the technique towards the intended direction of your throw. This is where the concept of tunnel and peripheral attitude relate to the execution of throwing techniques. If you maintain a peripheral attitude, you allow yourself the flexibility to feel the opponent's resistance and redirect your force to another angle where his balance is weak while using his resistance to help accomplish a throw.

Two concepts that illustrate the use of peripheral attitude when throwing are the concepts of Cutting the Circle and Continuing the Circle. Let's say we are attempting to execute a throwing technique on an attacker who is throwing a right punch. The defender escapes to angle # 4, inside the punch, and contacts the arm, manipulating it downward (Figure 140).

Figure 140

Figure 141

The defender then contacts or strikes the head to create an off-balancing effect or arching of the spine. The direction of this manipulation is outward beyond the foundation of the feet (Figure 141).

This outward manipulation pushes the attacker's triangle balance point to the defender's left leg. As the defender moves the leg to create a void for the attacker to fall into, he may feel the loss of balance and reposition his front foot out further in an attempt to catch his balance. In

Figure 142

Figure 143

doing so, the attacker will shift much of his weight forward to that balance catch point and resist from this point backward (Figure 142).

When feeling the resistance to this outward circular direction of the technique, the defender Cuts the Circle, manipulating the spine towards the back triangulation point to complete the throw (Figure 143).

This is just one example of Cutting the Circle. As you continue to experiment with the manipulation of an opponent's balance and structure, you will discover other applications for this concept.

Figure 144

Figure 145

Figure 146

Another concept that is useful in this aspect of the throwing arts, is Continuing the Circle. Assume we take the same situation of the attacker throwing a right punch, defender slipping to angle #4, and manipulating the arm and spine of attacker. As before, the defender then strikes/contacts the side of the head to arch the spine and manipulate the head out beyond the foundation of the feet, breaking the structure and balance of the attacker (Figure 145).

As in the prior example of Cutting the Circle, when the defender rotates to throw the off-balanced attacker, he repositions his right leg to catch his balance, making the throw to that angle improbable (Figure 146).

Feeling the resistance caused by the repositioning of the leg, the defender continues to rotate another 90 degrees while keeping the spinal structure arched, therefore creating another void for the attacker to fall into. (Figure 147)

Figure 147

The concepts of Cutting the Circle and Continuing the Circle are examples of maintaining a peripheral attitude while executing a self-defense technique. This state of mind is essential to being able to flow and adjust to changing circumstances and adjustments of an opponent.

Maintaining a peripheral attitude while executing a throwing technique allows the student to sense and feel the opponent's intention. Working with this concept also forces the student to look one step ahead when applying a technique, in order to see which way the opponent will resist in order to try to save his balance.

Everyday, we fight imbalance in the things we do without thinking about it. When you feel off-balance, your body naturally adjusts and pulls in the opposite direction to restore balance. This realization can help with understanding the strategy of an opponent whether it is one opponent or an army. Think of the philosophical applications this has in your life.

7) Proper triangulation and alignments

This reference is directed towards the student's triangulation. In order to have proper control and mass to apply in a technique, we must have proper triangulation.

This positioning also allows full use of all our weapons. Let's look at triangulation and how to align your self in relation to an opponent. Let's take the basic triangle of the upper body, with the shoulders being the back of the triangle and your hands forming the tip of the triangle (Figure 148). In this posture, your upper body is aligned so that your center is positioned behind the tip of your triangle. This is important for full use of both arms, for parrying incoming strikes, manipulation of attacker's structure and balance. This alignment also keeps the hips in a position for short, quick, rotations that contribute to maximum power for striking and manipulation. This triangle posture also allows for use of kicking with either leg, to help strike and destroy the structure of your opponent.

Figure 148

Figure 149

When we speak of aligning your triangles, look at the various points of alignment. The student first should see the triangle created by the shoulders to point of contact with the arms, shown in Figure 148.

Then notice how this upper body alignment also forms a triangle from the hara or navel area and third eye or forehead, to the point where the hands extend (Figure 149).

Other points of alignment would be the lower body triangles, hip-to-hip to point of contact with the arms, knees to point of contact, and feet to point of contact. Use these various checkpoints to help align your body, allowing for quicker response to an opponent's attacks, as well as better stability and power for striking and manipulation.

It is also important to realize that by positioning oneself behind the tip of a triangle, the opponent must strike around that point, causing him to widen the arc of his strike; while at the same time, allowing the defender the ability to respond with shorter, more direct movements.

Training Drills

In the following section we will cover some of the drills that I use in my school to convey the feeling and understanding of the concepts of throwing. These drills should be done slowly at first to see and feel the concepts and principles that we have covered to this point. Sensitivity and feel are extremely important. A student who rushes through these basic drills will miss the subtle things that contribute greatly to a deeper understanding of what we are studying.

Nagae Observation Drill

Have a training partner throw slow punches at you as you slip to different angles and reposition your body. Your training partner will punch slowly but extend through his intended target. Your focus should be on the imbalance that occurs on the initiation of the strike, middle of the strike, and end of the strike when the intended target is missed (overextension). After each punch is completed, your partner will have to readjust his gaze and mental focus, shift weight to initiate or start to throw the next strike, and rotate his center to hit his next intended target. Look at all the motion that is needed for your partner to accomplish his objective.

Your job is to look for ways to use his motion as well as the motion of his center during transition.

Molding Drill

This drill is done in a similar fashion as the Nagae Observation Drill, except this time your objective is to escape and blend with your attacker's movement, molding to his contour.

This drill serves several purposes. On one hand, the practitioner becomes more comfortable with escaping, giving up the space the attacker wants and finding new space to occupy. Also, because the idea of escaping requires the practitioner to stay relatively close to the attacker and

mold to him/her. As the practitioner molds to the attacker's body each time, he or she should contact different parts of the attacker's body with the hands, arms, and legs.

This gives the practitioner the ability to feel the attacker's preparatory, or loading motion to project the next strike. It is at these target areas where manipulation can take place.

In the following sequence of photos, you will see the defender is slipping through the attacker's punches. Each time the defender gives up the space the attacker is trying to fill with a punch, but stays relatively close to the attacker. Notice how the defender contacts different areas of the attacker's body.

This allows the defender the options of freezing the attacker's motion, speeding up the retracting side, stopping the projecting side, and also attacking the creases to disrupt the attacker's structure.

Fold-Arch-Throw Drill

This drill is one of the best tools I've found to convey the essential components of throwing to the student. When teaching, having a good physical vehicle to communicate the concepts and having the student actually feel the formula for creating a throw is priceless. In the performance of the Fold-Arch-Throw Drill, the student's eyes will be opened to the vast amount of options one has when it comes to the throwing arts. Once a student fully understands this drill, he/she can create an array of different throwing techniques using the formula taught by this drill.

The performance of this drill starts with attacking a simple crease of the elbow, which creates a fold in the body, then progresses to the manipulation of the spine to arch the body, taking the head out beyond the body's foundation, and finally directing the off-balanced body to an unsupported angle, creating the throw. In the following series of pictures, you'll find various techniques created using this simple drill. Take your time with this drill; communicate with your training partner and observe the effects on his body.

In Figure 150, the attacker has grabbed the lapel with his right hand. The defender creases the elbow (downward) with his left forearm to an angle unsupported by the attacker's leg, creating a slight fold of the body.

Figure 150

Figure 151

Figure 152

Figure 151 shows the defender immediately striking in an upward and backward angle. The strike stays connected to the face, arching the attacker, locking the spine, and placing the head out beyond the feet. Note: The defender must not allow the attacker to restore balance from the fold created

Figure 153

Figure 154

in Figure 150 as the upward strike is performed it will allow him to resist the arching strike.

In the last phase of this drill, (Figure 152) the defender directs the arched attacker to his backward triangulation point to complete the throw.

In the next sequence, we'll take the same attack and show how to create an entirely different technique using the same concept. In Figures 153 & 154, the attacker grabs the lapel with his right hand.

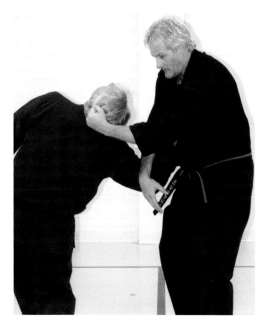

Figure 155

Figure 156

The defender checks the grabbing arm with the left hand while delivering a quick, off balancing strike to the attacker's face and continues into a downward strike to crease the elbow and fold his attacker. When creasing the elbow, be sure to manipulate downward and outward to an angle that the defender is not able to support. This will dramatically torque the spine and manipulate your attacker's center away from you.

After creating the fold, the defender reaches around to grab the hair in the back, opposite quadrant of the head. The defender then torques the neck, locking the spine and creating an arch by taking the attacker's head out beyond his feet (Figure 155).

After locking the spine and creating the arch, the defender steps behind with the left foot and rotates with the attacker taking him to the floor in Figure 156. The defender must keep the elbow creased during this process so the attacker stays unbalanced.

In the previous two sequences, we've shown the Fold-Arch-Throw Drill working from a grabbing attack because this situation is much easier to practice and to start to understand the concept from. But understand that the concept will work against all types of attack. In the next sequence, the attacker is punching to the head.

The concept is exactly the same. The defender starts with a lean to angle #3 to bait the attacker (Figure 157). (This is explained in the Leaning Factor portion of the Concepts Chapter.)

In Figure 158, the attacker throws a right punch to the defender's face. The defender shifts out to angle #4, escaping the path of the punch, while guiding the punching arm down with the left arm to fold the attacker.

This off-balancing parry must be done while the attacker is in motion, before he has a chance to regain his own structure. Immediately after creating the folding motion on the attacker, arch the head with a knife-hand or forearm strike (that stays connected) to arch and lock the spine (Figure 159).

Note that this arching motion must take the attacker's head out beyond his feet to eliminate any chance of restructuring for balance and resistance.

Figure 157

Figure 158

Figure 159

Figure 160

With the attacker's head and spine arched to this position, his balance is broken and he is in fact weightless for the throw. In Figure 160, the defender steps behind with his left leg and rotates the arched attacker towards an unsupported angle creating the throw.

In the last sequence, we'll look at the ability to use the Fold-Arch-Throw Drill to counter a joint lock attempt from the attacker.

In Figure 161, the attacker is attempting to apply an outward wristlock (kote geashi). As the attacker starts his motion to apply pressure to the joint, the defender speeds up and extends the attacker's intended circle of the locking motion, causing him to be off-balanced and folded. (Note how the defender automatically aligns his triangle when performing this action.) (Figure 162).

With the attacker folded, the defender strikes to the face to arch the head and spine backwards (Figure 163).

The defender moves his center towards the attacker's back triangulation point to complete the throw (Figure 164).

Figure 161

Figure 162

Figure 163

Figure 164

In the last couple of sequences we've tried to show some basic examples of the Fold-Arch-Throw Drill. Remember that this is only a drill. It's just a physical vehicle to feel and study the principles of throwing. The techniques that have been shown are just a few examples of a vast array of options. This drill is an excellent vehicle for the student to experiment and create different techniques.

Multiple Crease Throwing Drill

This is a great drill to use to explore the various creases as well as the effects they have on manipulating the body. Each crease of the body can be considered a weak link when attacked, to destroy the body's ability to maintain balance, or create resistance. The idea is to manipulate several creases of your partner's body, weakening his overall structure with each crease. Use this drill to experiment and observe how the manipulation of these creases, will set up, not only your throws, but also your strikes, locks, and escapes.

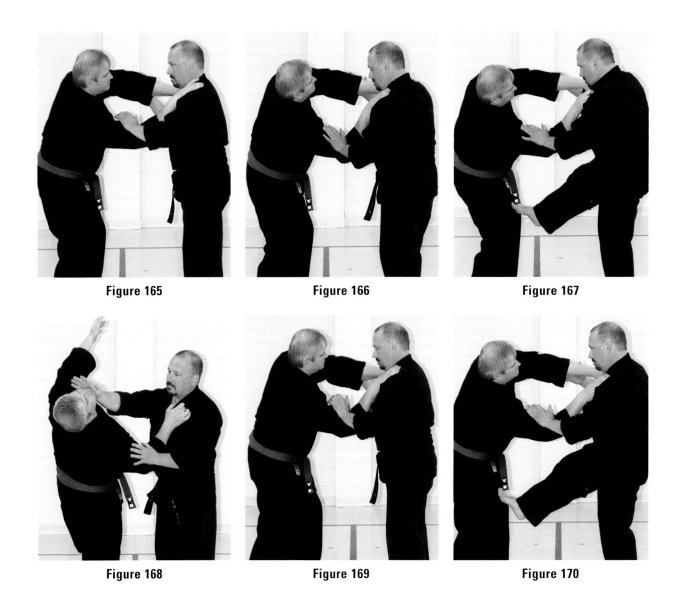

Figure 165

Figure 166

Figure 167

Figure 168

Figure 169

Figure 170

In Figure 165, the attacker executes a double choke on the defender.

The defender strikes down and inward to the elbow crease to create a fold and crease the knees slightly (Figure 166).

The defender then uses the foot to further manipulate the crease of the knee (Figure 167).

The defender follows up with a palm strike to the face, arching the head backwards creating the throw (Figure 168).

Then, experiment with changing the order of these creases. Attack the knee crease first, then follow with the elbow crease and strike the head to arch the spine.

Now, take these same basic creases and use them to bring the attacker's head in for the use of atemi waza.

Using the same attack, strike down into the elbow crease to buckle the knees and fold the body (Figure 169).

While maintaining the pressure and the fold of the elbow, strike the knee with a kick to further crease it, and bring the head in close for the application of atemi waza (Figure 170).

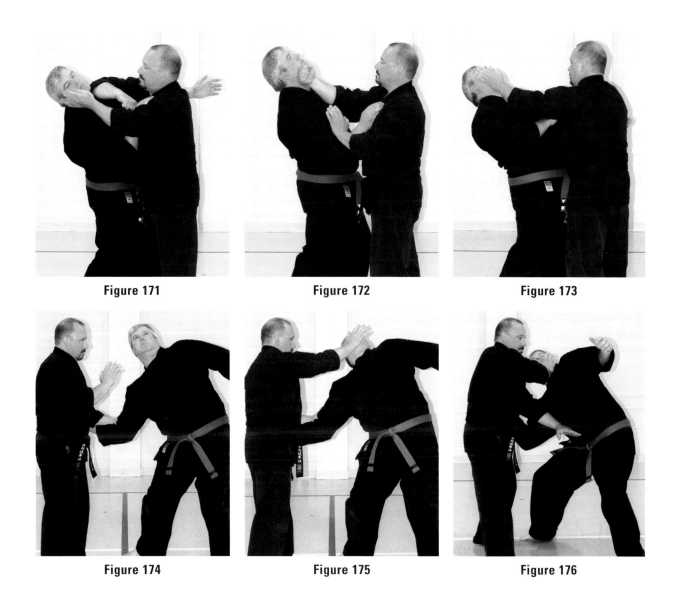

Figure 171   Figure 172   Figure 173

Figure 174   Figure 175   Figure 176

Immediately follow with a left palm heel and right elbow strike to the face (Figure 171).

Continue the combination by following with a right back fist strike (Figure 172).

Finish the combination with a left palm heel strike to the face, arching the attacker backwards into a throw (Figure 173).

In the next example, the attacker throws a right punch, the defender slips inside and parry blocks, manipulating the elbow and creating a slight fold (Figure 174).

While maintaining pressure on the elbow crease, the defender strikes the face with a palm heel strike, to arch the head and spine backwards, out beyond the feet (Figure 175).

As the attacker's upper body is arched back, the waist crease is brought forward and up. While maintaining the arch with the right hand, the defender strikes downward to the waist crease. This drives the attacker down and backward into a throw (Figure 176).

Study how the use of your locking arts can contribute to the refinement of creasing techniques. Experiment with various joint locks and observe their effects, and how proper application creates manipulation of other creases of the body. Take the effect created by the joint lock,

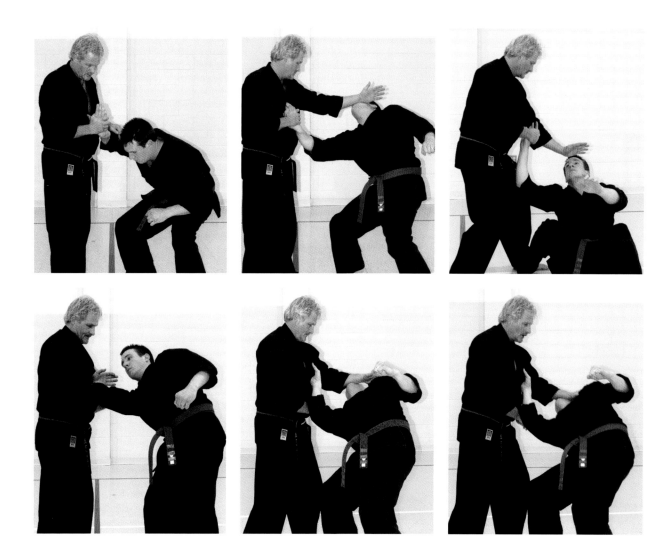

and identify and attack other applicable creases to totally destroy the balance and stability of the opponent.

Throwing is about creating imbalance. The more we learn about creating imbalance, the more effective our throwing arts will become. Think about ways to manipulate the opponent's balance, by destroying his structure.

Without structure and balance, an opponent's attack is rendered useless. Think about it— what if every time you reached to pick up an object, tried to take a step, threw a punch, or moved your body in any way, you were faced with losing your balance and falling down?

Much like a baby first learning to walk... how effective would you be?

Take the time to observe balance and imbalance—in order for an individual to move their body even in the simplest act of walking, balance must become imbalance followed by recovery. As Hanshi Bruce Juchnik told me when I first began studying Kempo, "Movement is a falling process." In order to move the body, stability must succumb to instability, and then regain stability. Is this not similar to one's path in life? In life, we become comfortable, and more stable in our environment, due to our ability to manage and control the things in it. When we face a new challenge or attempt to accomplish something new, we are somewhat imbalanced due to being in unexplored and unfamiliar territory. As we begin to understand and manage these new areas in our life, we become more confident and stable as a person. So, if movement is a falling process, imbalance due to failed attempts, and pain as a result of growth, all this must happen before we can become a more knowledgeable, well rounded individual. Look at the philosophical implications to our lives.

Look at the throwing arts in a different way. Work at understanding balance and imbalance, and your understanding of the throwing arts will deepen.

CHAPTER 11

Striking

Striking

One of the most dynamic aspects of the Kempo arts is their striking techniques. The Kempo stylist has the incredible ability to execute a myriad of lightning-fast hand combinations that come from different angles to overwhelm an opponent. An important thing to remember about striking—striking should serve two immediate purposes; not only does a strike make impact and cause external and internal damage, but it also destroys structure and balance, creating the inability to withstand follow-up strikes. Combination hitting should always be done with this frame of mind.

When using advanced Kosho Ryu striking, the strikes are directed to areas of the body that will manipulate the body structure, setting up the next strike and eventually removing all balance and therefore removing the ability to withstand the attack. This thinking follows the preparatory philosophy of Kosho Ryu Kempo.

Striking should always be done with a specific purpose in mind. That's not to say that your purpose cannot change if you run into difficulty. Striking can be done for several reasons.

I like to think of the different philosophies or mindsets of striking as off-balancing, manipulating, void-filling, and destructive striking. Let's first look at this from a philosophical approach to life.

It is important to understand that our timing, approach, and delivery of what actions we take in life, must be in accordance with that which is needed at that specific time. There are times when a forceful and assertive mind-set is what the situation requires. Then, there are times when a passive mind-set will accomplish more. It all depends on the situation, and the emotions and point of view of the people we're dealing with at the time.

A very important aspect of this is the understanding of the other party. Whether it be an opponent, a business associate, or a person involved in your personal life, we must develop an understanding of them. The better we understand them—their moral convictions, their emotions, what's most important to them—the better our chances of winning or succeeding at what we set out to accomplish.

So, if we take this philosophy towards life, we must apply the same principles to our martial arts, and in this case our striking. In the following pages, we'll look at how and where to apply our off-balancing, manipulating, void filling, and destructive/ finishing strikes.

Figure 177

Figure 178

Figure 179

Figure 180

First, a strike can be done simply to off-balance an opponent mentally and physically enable the defender to escape. In figure 177, the attacker is moving in with a right punch, when the defender sees motion, he angles off slightly to the right while throwing a left strike to the position where the attacker is moving towards (center pole of the octagon), making him react to the strike and arching him backwards. This off-balances the attacker, allowing the defender a total escape (Figure 178).

The use of striking to off-balance an attacker, mentally and physically, when in a grabbing situation is essential for accomplishing a total escape. In Figure 179, the defender strikes with a finger thrust to the throat notch, forcing the attacker to arch backwards and release his double choke. As this mental/ physical off balance takes place, the defender can now accomplish a total escape or engage the opponent (Figure 180).

When using strikes to manipulate the attacker's body, remember they are used in order to: #1) manipulate or set up the attacker for the next strike and/or #2) to manipulate the body structure so the attacker can not use balance and stability to withstand a blow.

When using striking to set up the body for follow-up strikes, it is important to understand the creases of the body and how they can be used to manipulate the body structure to accomplish this purpose. Some simple examples of this follow.

In this first sequence, the attacker throws a right punch and the defender slips to angle #4 on the inside of the punch, and performs a parry block (Figure 181).

Figure 181

Figure 182

Figure 183

Using the left (and closest) hand, the defender strikes upward to the face with a palm heel strike as the attacker rotates, causing him to be arched backward (Figure 182).

Because of the backward arch of the upper body, the waist crease area becomes arched forward to be struck with a downward punch towards the attacker's back triangulation point (Figure 183).

In the next sequence, the attacker throws a right punch and the defender slips/escapes to angle #4, inside of the punch (Figure 184).

As the attacker shifts to initiate a second punch, the defender strikes downward and inward with a punch to the waist crease (Figure 185).

This strike creases the waist and brings the head down and into a vulnerable position.

When the attacker's body structure is manipulated so that the head is down and forward, the defender immediately follows with a left palm strike and right punch. (Figure 186) This com-

Figure 184

Figure 185

Figure 186

| Figure 187 | Figure 188 | Figure 189 |

bination continues with a right elbow strike, right back fist strike, and left palm heel (Figures 187-189).

Now, let's look at an example of using strikes to manipulate the structure of an opponent so that his ability to absorb or take a finishing destructive blow is diminished or destroyed. Before dissecting the attack and defense, remember, when we are feeling balanced in our daily lives, we feel stronger and more capable of handling the challenges and battles of daily life. But when we are feeling out of balance, we seem to lack the strength, confidence, and commitment to handle things as well. That's not to say that we don't handle or deal with them, but we encounter more difficulty. Much the same is true with how an opponent receives a strike. If his body structure is balanced, he may be able to absorb the strike; he may be able to move with ease to avoid the strike. Neither of these scenarios is what we want to happen.

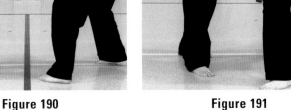

In Figure 190, the attacker begins to throw a right punch; the defender is leaning to angle #4 in a preparatory manner to bait the attacker and allow for an easier transition to escape.

In Figure 191, as the punch is delivered, the defender slips out to angle #3 (outside of the arm) and performs a parry block to slightly manipulate structure and align the triangle.

| Figure 190 | Figure 191 |

As the attacker rotates center to throw a left punch, the defender strikes the weightless attacker with a quick right punch causing the attacker's spine to arch. This strike removes the attacker's ability to absorb any strike due to the manipulation of his structure (Figure 192).

In Figure 193, the defender performs a male percussion strike (otoko no atemi) on a weakened opponent. Striking to an opponent in this position can cause an extreme amount of damage.

Note that otoko no atemi will be discussed further later in this chapter.

Void filling strikes are used essentially to fill in gaps or spaces in our defenses especially when we are in transition from one position to the next, during an avoidance or escaping motion.

These strikes allow us the time we need by intercepting the attacker's motion and occupying the center pole of the octagon (neutral space between attacker and defender).

Figure 194, shows the defender slipping inside the right punch of the attacker. Note the attacker will immediately fill the void in the defender's defenses. If the defender is to

Figure 192

Figure 193

Figure 194

Figure 195

Figure 196

Figure 197

Figure 198   **Figure 199**   **Figure 200**

stay ahead of the attacker's tempo, he must dominate the timing by using a void filling strike to offset the attacker.

In Figure195, the attacker throws a right punch and the defender escapes to angle #4 (inside of the punch). Note the hand posture of the defender, using proper triangulation.

In Figure 196, as the attacker starts to rotate his body to throw the left punch, the defender shifts to the left (angle #3) and strikes the face with a left palm strike to fill the void and allow for a follow up strike with a right punch. The defender then follows with the desired hand combination to finish the opponent (Figure 197).

Let's look at another example of using a void filling strike. In Figure 198, the defender slips outside the attacker's right punch (angle #3), performs a parry block and aligns triangles.

As the attacker rotates to throw the left punch, the defender throws a right punch to fill the void and intercept the attacker's motion (Figure 199). With the attacker in an off-balanced state, the defender finishes with a left punch (Figure 200).

Destructive finishing strikes are exactly that–strikes that are meant to finish the confrontation. While some of these other strikes will finish an opponent whose structure has been totally taken away, destructive finishing strikes are generally power strikes. Strikes such as a powerful gyaku tsuki or reverse punch (Figure 201 & 202) would fit into this category.

Figure 201   **Figure 202**

These strikes are male in nature and will be discussed in the section of ototko no atemi or male percussion striking.

An important factor to remember is that all of the different strikes that we have discussed are applied on an opponent who is in rotation or frozen in a posture that allows for easy destruction. When an attacker is in rotation, from one structured posture to another, he is weak while in transition and does not have the ability to resist or absorb the strike. If the attacker is also placed in a frozen position at an angle to which he is vulnerable, the defender's strikes will have maximum efficiency. Therefore we must use the mindset that for our striking to be effective, we must first manipulate to weaken the structure, creating a target that is in acceptance to our strikes.

Onna No Atemi

Onna No Atemi or, female percussion striking, uses multiple upper body strikes which come from a variety of angles to overwhelm and destroy an opponent. These combinations must be done in quick, tight combinations to avoid creating a void for the opponent to fill.

As we have discussed in several areas of this book, any technique, including striking, throwing, or locking, requires proper escaping and triangulation to be effective. Through the use of proper escaping, we create the need for the attacker to readjust his/her mental and physical energies. This re-adjustment causes imbalance mentally and physically. The physical imbalance is created through rotation of the body. A weightless state is created in moving from one position to the next.

The use of proper triangulation goes hand-in-hand with the use of proper escaping. Proper triangulation is used to position the body, and to set up the hands for quick, direct, and powerful striking. This positioning is also very important in order to parry and redirect further attacks from the opponent while manipulating his or her body structure.

   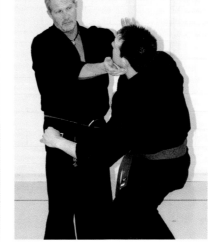   

Figure 203   **Figure 204**   **Figure 205**

When using the concept of triangulation to set up the hands, it is extremely important to direct the tip of our triangle in the direction we choose to accept. For instance, if we want to strike at the attacker's center, our triangle should be directed in line with that center (Figure 203).

The body is pre-positioned for engagement, so the defender can attack immediately as the opponent's rotation causes a weightless state.

This allows the defender to strike effectively to the opponent's center, by using just a slight rotation of the hip (Figure 204).

If we choose to attack the opponent's head or face from the outside, striking in towards the center, our hands form a triangle with the target with the forward hand along side the head (Figure 205).

This action is performed after the defender's parry block and manipulation of the arm. Positioning the hand in this area places it in a blind spot, so the strike comes from outside the attacker's visual plane. In Figure 206, the defender manipulates the hip, by rotating the toes of

Figure 206

Figure 207

Figure 208

Figure 209

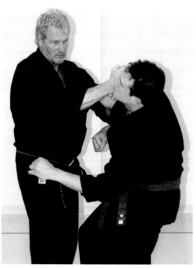

Figure 210

Figure 211   **Figure 212**

the right foot inward, striking the side of the face as the attacker becomes weightless on the secondary rotation. This strike would offset the structure of the attacker, whereby the defender follows up with an onna no atemi combination (Figures 207-212).

Another variation of this technique would be slipping to the inside of the right punch, parry blocking and directing the triangle towards the outside of attacker's head, contacting the shoulder (Figure 213).

As the attacker rotates, retracting the right arm, the defender rotates the hip inward, and strikes the side of head/face with an inward palm strike (Figure 214). This strike is delivered when the attacker is in a weightless state, and is followed with an onna hand combination (Figures 215 - 218).

Figure 213   **Figure 214**   **Figure 215**

| **Figure 216** | **Figure 217** | **Figure 218** |

Using a preparatory mindset when positioning the hands for use in striking is extremely important. Experiment and make it a point to learn how different areas of the body react to different strikes. Then practice subtle, hand positioning following blocks and parries.

Note how this allows ease in performing various void filling strikes that are quick, direct, and important for intercepting an opponent's motion.

Let's take a look at some various examples of preparatory hand placement after the initial parry or entry. Place the hand outside the visual plane of the head as in Figure 219. Strike inward with the heel of the palm to weak areas of the face/head, as the attacker begins to rotate (Figure 220).

Devastating strikes can be targeted towards areas of the body projected towards you. In Figure 221, after blocking from the outside of the arm, the hand is placed in a direct line with the retracted shoulder.

| **Figure 219** | **Figure 220** | **Figure 221** |

As this shoulder projects to throw the second punch, the muscle groups will be opening, therefore allowing for a much more penetrating, effective punch to the incoming shoulder (Figure 222).

Another example of this strategy would be to counterattack the projecting hip of an attacker as he rotates to throw the second punch (Figure 223).

Figure 222 **Figure 223**

Building an Arsenal

When attempting to put together several strikes into an onna no atemi waza, we must remember that the combination must have continuity and flow to gain maximum effectiveness, and must be tightly constructed to eliminate voids for the attacker to fill during execution. Look at how the body rotates, and see how the rotation of the spine extends or swings the arms towards the intended target. Also recognize there are several weapons to strike with on each arm. These work in conjunction with each other. Instead of striking just once with each arm, use all the weapons available on a single arm when striking. Let's look at some basic examples of this.

The defender has slipped inside the attacker's right punch and aligned his triangles for engagement (Figure 224).

The defender then strikes on the attacker's next rotation, using a simultaneous left palm heel and right punch to the attacker's jaw (Figure 225).

The defender continues to rotate, following the punch with a right elbow strike (Figure 226), and then reverses the rotation by retracting the right hip, to hit with a right back fist, to opposite side of the head (Figure 227).

Figure 224 **Figure 225**

Figure 226

Figure 227

Figure 228

The defender would then finish the combination with a left palm heel (Figure 228).

Make note of how the rotation of the spine not only projects the strike, but causes a counter retraction of the opposite arm. Too often, we think only of striking with the projecting motion and do nothing with the retracting motion of the arm.

Let's look at another combination using the same guidelines. In this combination, the defender has entered inside the attacker's right punch, parrying with the right hand, and positioning the right elbow for the initial strike (Figure 229).

On the attacker's second rotation, the defender strikes the incoming shoulder with the right elbow (Figure 230) to stop the projecting side.

Figure 229

Figure 230

Figure 231

Figure 232

Figure 233

Figure 234

Figure 235

Immediately following the elbow strike to the shoulder, the defender projects a right back fist strike to the side of the attacker's head (Figure 231) and a left palm strike (Figure 232). This is followed by a right punch (Figure 233), elbow (Figure 234), and back fist (Figure 235).

Otoko No Atemi

Otoko no atemi, or male percussion striking, uses the connection of upper and lower body centers, along with proper triangulation, as well as proper skeletal and muscular structure to produce maximum destruction to an opponent. This strike can be totally effective whether the opponent is in either a weightless state (in rotation), or in a frozen state.

The use of male percussion striking is often executed with the use of a long, wide base, such as a zenkutsu dachi or front stance. Using a wider base to deliver a strike results in maximum torque and power. Having time to employ a strike using a wide base requires the practitioner to have

Figure 236

Figure 237

either already escaped to an angle (requiring the opponent to rotate to find him), or to have placed his opponent in a manipulated, frozen position, from which he cannot withstand the strike.

As discussed before, the escaping arts are incredibly important to achieving maximum efficiency in one's striking, throwing, and locking arts. If the practitioner wishes to strike a weightless opponent with a male percussion strike, he must reposition himself to an angle that requires the opponent to rotate and cross his own center. The practitioner also must immediately align his triangles, allowing for maximum efficiency and effectiveness of the strike. This escaping, or repositioning allows the practitioner the time needed to set the base, aligning triangles, and executing the rotation for the male strike.

An example of this would be for the defender to escape to the outside of the attacker's right punch and align triangles (Figure 236). From this triangulated position, the defender is loaded and ready to execute a strike. As the attacker rotates to strike, the male percussion strike is delivered. (Figure 237)

Take the needed time to experiment with your striking. Strike to different areas of the body. And notice the effects. How does the opponent react?

Experiment with strikes to various joints. What structural imbalances do they create? How can strikes to certain areas of the body distort and manipulate, setting up other striking combinations or throwing techniques?

Start to develop an eye, and an understanding of the opponent's body mechanics and how they react to various strikes.

Study the following photos for a simple example of this.

The use of a downward strike to the waist crease causes the pelvis to move down and away. This motion brings the head and neck, down and in, for closer attack. In Figure 238, the defender has slipped to the outside of the attacker's punch, parried and aligned triangles. As the attacker rotates, the defender strikes the waist crease, bringing the attacker's head in for attack (Figure 239).

Figure 238

Figure 239

Figure 240

Figure 241

Figure 242

The defender immediately follows with a right elbow strike (Figure 240), a right back fist (Figure 241), and a left palm heel strike (Figure 242). The manipulation caused by the strike to the waist crease, allows for a devastating combination.

Look at all the tools you have at your disposal. How can the practitioner use the locking/manipulation of an opponent's joints to destroy structure and balance, while setting up important areas of the body for further attack?

Experiment with the various joint locks you are familiar with. Notice how manipulation of these joints causes various effects on the body. How can you use your striking to take advantage of this? Learn to take the effect of the joint manipulation and use it to make your striking incredibly effective. Study the following sequence of photos.

Take this same area of thinking, and look at the effects caused by various throwing techniques. Use the principles/concepts to create structural imbalance for your throwing arts. Have you ever had a throwing technique go bad? We've all had a training partner who has caught

his balance or re-structured slightly, causing our technique to fall short. But most likely your technique created somewhat of an off-balancing effect. Take the effect caused by it, and employ your striking arts to finish the confrontation. This would be demonstrating the use of a peripheral mindset. In other words, don't be so singularly focused on your intended manipulation that you lose sight of other possibilities.

Yet, another area to study would be application of the pressure points of the body. Learn how to strike in between the muscle groups, to penetrate and activate the pressure points. Study how certain muscle groups are opening during an attacker's movement, and others are closing. Striking these areas of the body that are opening allows the practitioner to get the maximum effect from his strikes.

Study the reactions and effects of striking to the creases of the body. Experiment with striking these creases to various angles of the octagon, and observe the effect. As you do this, the doors will continue to open, and you will gain a better understanding of how and why to implement your striking arts.

CHAPTER 12

Kata

The Study of Kata

In the context of Kosho, kata is a pre-arranged form of fundamental martial components, and is one of the core training devices in many systems. These components include stances, blocks, strikes, and kicks. These pre-arranged patterns are used to teach many aspects of the martial arts.

The history of kata can be traced back to a form called The 18 Hands of Lohan. The great Bodhidharma in 527 BC taught this form to the Shaolin monks of China. The word kata, which is translated to "form," comes from the Okinawan lineage of karate. Although the kata of Okinawa are just several hundred years old, the Chinese arts which laid the foundation for Okinawan karate have forms that date back much further.

The premise of a form or formula, which allows a person to memorize and practice, has been around since the beginning of time and is not necessarily unique to the martial arts. The simple task of building a fire for preparing food is a process that could be considered a kata or form as it is a sequence of tasks that need to be performed in a certain order.

Anytime we have a procedure, which has certain purpose in mind, we organize the components and arrange them in the proper order to create a formula by which to memorize and practice them. In doing so, we create a kata.

In the early stages, kata training takes the practitioner through his or her basic fundamentals, while moving through a pattern comprised of various angles and directions. This takes the student through the progression of practicing basic fundamentals from a still or standing position, to one of movement and motion. This allows the practitioner to work his stances and transitions, along with the proper timing for blocks and strikes.

Kata also is used as a tool to enhance the practitioner's visualization of possible attackers, their positioning, along with various target areas on an opponent. This visualization training allows the student to execute his fundamentals with focus, speed, power and intensity, without the threat of being struck, or doing harm to another individual. Although kata is a solo practice, it must be done with the assumption of the attacker's positioning and aggressive movement directed towards the practitioner.

The student must then practice and repeat the form until he or she has no need to think about the pattern or the techniques. This allows the student to combine focus, speed, power, timing and intensity in his form. This is the point where the student begins to project his own attitude and spirit while performing the kata.

In the physical sense, kata is an excellent tool to forge the practitioner's body. Repetition of kata helps build strength, coordination, balance and proper breath control. Just as a piece of steel must be forged to become a katana, or sword, so the body must go through this process.

Strength Training & Application Training

The performance of kata should be looked at in two ways—strength training and application training. Strength training in the performance of kata is accomplished through the use of large movement and motion. The stance work in kata for strength training should be that of long, deep, powerful stances. Although the transition from one stationary posture to the next is difficult from these deep stances, the practitioner strengthens the legs and hip region of the body. All upper body movement, such as blocking and striking techniques, is performed with large, powerful motion.

Application training in the performance of kata, is done with shorter stances, allowing the practitioner to move more freely from stance to stance. The upper body movements are executed in a more compact manner. Blocks and strikes are more direct, eliminating any extraneous motion, while keeping the body aligned properly. This allows the practitioner a more direct and effective application of his technique. Note that this is done to allow the practitioner a more efficient technique, which does not allow for voids, which the opponent will attempt to fill.

It is important to understand that strength training should be done before application training. As with learning any new physical activity, one must start with larger motion. Larger, more elongated motion is easier for the practitioner to observe and replicate. As we become more adept at that physical activity, we find ways to sharpen and refine the motion. Hence, in the refinement process, we learn to eliminate excess motion and become more direct with our application. Take the time to apply this approach to your kata, and all your physical activity.

Kata as a Tool for Studying Motion

Another aspect of kata that many people over look: kata is an excellent tool for studying movement from one posture to another. This can be referred to as transitional motion. Transitional motion is the loading of energy in the muscle groups that allows a practitioner to repel from one stance or posture, to the next. In order to move from a settled stance or posture, we must overcome gravity to initiate movement in our next intended direction. Kata is a wonderful tool for this study. In order to do this, the practitioner must slow down, and notice what muscle groups will allow the body to repel from the current stance. This may be a shifting of the hips, a repositioning or rotation of a foot, a tensing of a certain muscle group, or a manipulation of the arms, which will allow for unrestricted adjustment and movement in our new intended direction.

Let's look at a specific movement from the kata Pinan Shodan. In the transition from the

Figure 247

Figure 248

Figure 249

second to third move, the practitioner has stepped forward with the right foot into zenkutsu dachi or front stance, and punched with the right hand (Figure 247).

The practitioner must repel from this posture, stepping behind with the right leg, and pivot his center 180 degrees to execute a low block (Figure 248).

Since the practitioner has a greater portion of his weight on the forward leg, and the right hip is projected, there must be a retraction on the right hip and a body shift backwards to allow proper weight distribution for the turn and block. This retraction and weight shift must happen immediately after the punch reaches full extension, to eliminate any pause in the practitioner's movement.

Place yourself in this stance and execute your right punch. Now slowly make the transition to the next posture. Feel all the motion needed to repel and move to the next position.

The idea is for the practitioner to automatically adjust the body before taking the actual step behind to turn to the opposite direction.

This is preparatory motion. It is the initial body repositioning, which allows for a quicker, more balanced transition to the next move.

The use of kata is invaluable, as a vehicle to experiment and understand how the body moves, and especially, how preparatory manipulation of the body structure enhances economy in motion. Take the time to look deeper into your kata. Learn to slow down, and observe motion, especially the transitions from one move to the next. Let the kata be your teacher, helping you gain a better understanding of how you may move more efficiently, and move on time.

Bunkai

The term bunkai, can be translated to analysis or interpretation. When we analyze our kata, we must take several factors into consideration. First, we have to understand that our opponent is not a stationary, stagnant target; your opponent will not just throw the first strike and just stand there, waiting for you to counter and apply your designated self-defense technique. Realize that your opponent is a living, breathing, moving body that will adapt and adjust to environmental changes and stimuli.

Another aspect for consideration when analyzing kata, is your opponent's timing and distance, and the angle from which they are attacking. Realize that in the performance of a technique in your kata, the timing and distancing of an opponent may change, as well as your timing and distancing.

Realize that the contact points of your technique must change to accommodate this variable.

In the previous photos, the defender's timing is delayed, so the shuto or knife hand strike must be used to intercept or block the incoming strike (Figure 250)

In Figure 251, the defender's timing is enhanced, due to proper visual contact, allowing him to move on the attacker's initial motion, striking to the face of the incoming attacker.

In another example of this, the opponent's attack is coming from a side angle. With proper timing and distance, the defender strikes with a shuto to the face as the attacker enters (Figure 252). In the same circumstance, but from a shorter distance, the defender strikes first with the el-

Figure 250

Figure 251

Figure 252

Figure 253

Figure 254

bow (Figure 253) to intercept the attacker's motion, then continues with a shuto strike to the face (Figure 254). This is an example of using the different contact points of the knife hand motion.

In the analysis of kata, we must look at the motion of the desired technique. Pay attention to the motion of your blocking techniques. May they be used to intercept and manipulate the structure of the opponent, placing them in an off-balanced state, for further destruction through strikes? How can the practitioner employ the blocking motion to control the attacker through the utilization of throwing and locking techniques? These are some of the aspects we need to think about, and experiment with, in our analysis of kata.

Bunkai Examples of Kata

In this section, we will look at some moves in kata, and explore some variations for their use. The individual moves selected are from kata that are widely practiced by many systems in the hope that the reader will be able to apply them to their own studies.

The first technique is the opening move to Pinan #1. The general explanation for this move is that the arms are brought up in preparation to block (Figure 255). The practitioner then turns to his immediate left, stepping out into front leaning stance, blocking a front thrust kick from the attacker. (Figure 256).

Figure 255

Figure 256

An alternative explanation for this move would be that of being grabbed by an attacker in front of you. In the first variation of this move, the defender brings the right arm up between the arms of the attacker, driving the forearm down to crease the elbow joint. This creasing motion buckles the knees of the attacker, and folds his body forward. The left arm then comes around to grab the hair of the attacker, twisting the head to lock and arch the spine (Figure 257).

Figure 257

Figure 258

Figure 259

The defender then steps out with the left foot, removing a balance point from the attacker, and executes a throw (Figures 258 and 259). Perform this throwing technique with extreme caution!

Let's look at another variation of this technique. The defender can, after folding the attacker's structure from striking the elbow crease. Bring the left arm across in front of the head, striking and extending the arm. The defender then arches the attacker's spine, while keeping the attacker's elbow close to his body and steps out to execute the throw.

(Figures 260, 261, and 262)

Figure 260

Figure 261

Figure 262

Figure 263

Figure 264

Figure 265

Figure 266

Figure 267

The next move we'll cover is the opening move to Pinan #2 (Nidan). The general explanation for this move is this: an attacker who is to the full left of the defender throws a punch to the face, while the defender pivots into a back stance, and blocks the punch (Figures 263 and 264)

An alternative explanation of this kata technique would be a frontal confrontation with an attacker. In this case, the attacker has grabbed the lapel with one hand, to stabilize, punching with the other hand. The defender blocks the punch with the rising motion of the right arm (Figure 265).

After blocking the punch, the defender strikes with his left forearm into the elbow fold of the attacker's grabbing arm, and simultaneously strikes the head with a right hammer fist (Figure 266).

The defender then finishes with a left hammer fist strike to the temple. (Figure 267).

This bunkai combines the second and third moves of Pinan Nidan.

Figure 268

Figure 269

Figure 270

Figure 271

The kata Seisan has a move where the practitioner settles into a stance and punches, then shifts backward to a neko ashi dach, or cat stance, and executes a middle block.

The general explanation for this move is simply that the practitioner shifts back to avoid and block the punch (Figures 268 and 269). Another interpretation of this move would be that the arm extended to punch has been grabbed by an opponent (Figure 270). The defender then circles the hand around to grab and control the attacker's arm, then shifts in a backward direction, which hyper extends the elbow. The chudan uke, or middle block is used to destroy the elbow joint (Figure 271).

Jodan Age Uke—High Block

Chudan Soto Uke—Inside Middle Block

Chudan Uke—Outside Middle Block

Gedan Barai—Downward Block

Realize that any blocking motion that you perform, can be applied as a joint manipulation. Look at the following photos to see the various blocking motions and how to use them for joint manipulation.

The Naihanchi kata is a widely practiced form, done by many different arts. Choki Motobu, who is said to have performed it 500 times a day, made this kata famous.

Figure 272

Figure 273

Figure 274

Figure 275

Let's look at the first several moves of the Naihanchi kata. The general explanation of these moves starts with the defender blocking a punch from the side (Figure 272). The defender then grabs the attacker and pulls him into an elbow strike (Figure 273).

The next move has the practitioner chambering the hands, in preparation to block (Figure 274). Another attacker at the full left, throws a front kick. The defender blocks it with a downward parry (Figure 275).

Another interpretation of these moves would assume the opponent is attacking from the front right 45-degree angle. This is a close range situation.

Figure 276

Figure 277

Figure 278

Figure 279

Figure 280

The defender intercepts the attacker's punch, with a right ridge hand strike. Note that this block/strike intercepts the incoming strike, off-balancing the opponent and draws him in close to the defender (Figure 276). The defender follows immediately with an elbow strike (Figure 277).

The defender then drops the arms into a chambered position on the right hip. This motion drops or settles the attacker's weight. (Figure 278). The defender then strikes the midsection, with a motion of a low block (Figure 279) and a punch (Figure 280).

Let's look at another explanation for the chambered catch position, low block and cross-punch.

In Figure 281, the attacker has grabbed the defender's right wrist. The defender rolls around the outside of the attacker's arm to grab and secure his arm. This motion is augmented by the left hand (Figure 282).

The defender strikes the extended arm of the attacker, which drops the body weight and folds the attacker forward, exposing the head for attack (Figure 283). This strike may be targeting the extended elbow of the attacker, or may strike the pressure point known as Triple Warmer #12 located in the area of the triceps muscle. Pressure points will be further discussed in the next chapter.

The defender then executes a cross-punch to the side of the attacker's head (Figure 284).

Figure 281

Figure 282

Figure 283

Figure 284

Pressure Points in Kata

The recognition and use of pressure points contained in kata is an invaluable tool for the practitioner's study. As mentioned in the chapter on Kyusho-Jitsu, the use of pressure points in kata, allows the practitioner to visualize striking and manipulating specific targets for their movements in kata. Study of the location, and the angle and direction of these points, will enhance the practitioner's insight and interpretation, giving them a more profound meaning of the moves in kata.

In this chapter, we have tried to give the reader avenues in which to study their kata or forms. True study requires deep and probing concentration. One must look at things from many perspectives. For a practitioner to truly see, they must first have an open mind, free from prejudice, opinion, and ego. Look at your kata in this manner, and you will find an invaluable tool for many areas of study within your martial art.

CHAPTER 13

Pressure Points

Kyusho-Jitsu Pressure Point Attacking

A very important tool to have in one's arsenal as a martial artist is knowledge of pressure points and how to apply them. The study of Kyusho-Jitsu is vast, one that a student can spend a lifetime researching and practicing—although this is also true of all the other aspects of the martial arts.

Pressure point knowledge is an important part of being an effective martial artist. It is not an end unto itself, but rather a means to an end. It is an important part of the study of the whole.

The study of Kyusho-Jitsu can be used to enhance a student's training in many different ways. Studying the location of pressure points on the body teaches the student a great deal about an opponent's anatomy and makes the student more aware of the body's weaknesses.

This study has to include the proper angle and direction needed to activate the points, as well as how and where the points lie in between the muscle groups. Understand that pressure points lie on energy pathways or meridians, of which the points are the access spots of these meridians.

Another important aspect of this study is experimenting and understanding how the body reacts to the different strikes or manipulations of these points. This is extremely important to operating in a preparatory state of mind, allowing the defender to manipulate the attacker to set up the next move, whether it is a strike, lock, or throw. For example, many pressure point strikes or manipulations will cause a creasing of certain joints, which in turn contributes to the destruction of the opponent's structure or balance.

This manipulation or destruction of the structure eliminates the opponent's ability to absorb a strike, creating maximum damage when hit. It also eliminates the ability to resist a throwing technique. It all goes back to balance; maintain your structure and balance while eliminating your opponent's!

The study of Kyusho-Jitsu also significantly enhances a practitioner's targeting ability. When studying and practicing to strike and manipulate pressure points, the student must target those strikes and grabs with pinpoint accuracy. This practice requires the practitioner to attack

points that are located along the edges of bones, in the creases between muscle groups, and in cavity areas. In doing so, the practitioner's targeting abilities are greatly enhanced and focused towards efficient, effective strikes to vulnerable areas of the body.

This mindset of striking/manipulating with pinpoint accuracy also enhances the practitioner's visualization skills when working any solo aspect of martial arts training. This training is especially helpful in kata training. Performing kata with focus and intensity is difficult sometimes, due to the student's inability to visualize what and where the motion is directed.

Pressure point instruction greatly enhances the practitioner's visualization of these moves, allowing for better focus and intensity.

Basic Pressure Points of the Hand & Arm

TRIPLE WARMER #3 (TW-3)

TW–3 is located on the back of the hand, approximately 1/3 of the way from the knuckles to the wrist, in between the bones of the ring finger and the pinky finger. This point responds best to a pressing application.

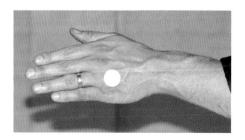

This point (TW-3) is attacked with the thumb during the execution of a Kotegaeshi, or outward wristlock. Using this point creates pain and helps weaken and crease the wrist for application of the lock.

LUNG #10 (L-10)

This point (L-10) is located about mid-point of the first metacarpal, in the meat of the thumb, just underneath the bone. L-10 responds best to direct finger pressure.

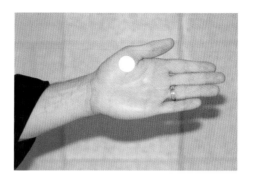

This point can be used in conjunction with TW-3 when applying an outward wristlock (kotegaeshi).

When using the two prior points (TW-3 and LU-10) in a wristlock application, notice the folds and creases created in the body's structure.

HEART #6 (H-6)

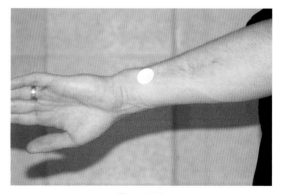

This point is located approximately 1/2 AU, or about a quarter of an inch, up from the wrist crease on the inside of the forearm. Pressing this point into the forearm causes the opponent's wrist and grip to weaken.

Heart #6

LUNG #8 (L-8)

This point is located approximately one AU up from the wrist crease on the thumb side of the inside of the forearm. Use this point in conjunction with Heart #6.

Use Heart #6 and Lung #8 to create pain and weaken the wrist in a grabbing situation. These points will allow the practitioner to release the grab.

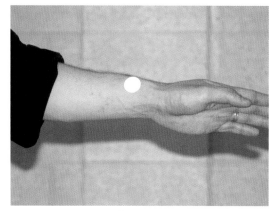

Lung #8

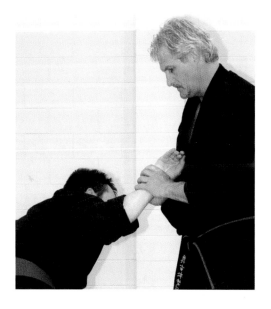

TRIPLE WARMER #11 (TW-11)

TW-11 is located approximately 2 AU (1 inch) above the tip of the elbow on the tricep's tendon. When attacking this point, place the palm on the elbow tip, and fold the fingers into a fist, digging the knuckles into the tendon and rub in an up and down manner.

One self-defense application for attacking TW-11 is performed from a cross wrist grab. In Figure 285, the defender steps to the outside of attacker's strength (angle #3), and circles the hand around to grab the forearm to stabilize and rotate the elbow upward for attack.

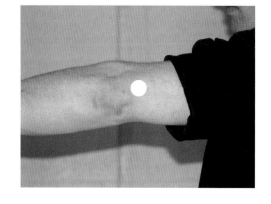

The defender then places his palm on the elbow point and rolls the knuckles into TW-11. Digging the knuckles in and rubbing in an up and down manner, while applying upward pressure with the lower part of the arm for increased pain.

Figure 285   Figure 286

TRIPLE WARMER #12 (TW- 12)

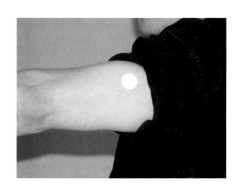

TW-12 is located in the middle of the triceps muscle. Striking this point into the bone causes the shoulder to release, and the elbow to be locked, as well as the knees to buckle.

In the next sequence, the attacker grabs the left wrist with his right hand. (Figure 287) The defender rolls the grabbed hand around the outside of the grabbing arm and secures the attacker's forearm, and rotates the left hip back to hyperextend the attacker's elbow. (Note: make sure to rotate the arm to position TW-12 upward, for ease in striking.) (Figure 288).

The defender then strikes downward to TW-12, hitting with the bone of the forearm. Remember to use your weight, settling into this strike...hit with the body, not just with the arm (Figure 289).

Figure 287   Figure 288   Figure 289

LUNG #6 (L-6)

L-6 is located on the inside of the forearm, approximately halfway from the wrist to the forearm. This point responds best to a striking motion.

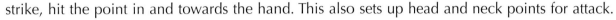

When striking L-6, use a weapon such as a knife hand or the boney edge of a forearm, angling into the point and back towards the hand. Striking this point causes pain and numbness in the arm and the release of the fist.

Using the retracting motion of the knife hand strike, hit the point in and towards the hand. This also sets up head and neck points for attack.

Next, take the projecting motion of the knife hand, and strike STOMACH #9 into the neck. (Refer to ST #9 for placement of this point.) Using this application lends much more meaning to a shuto or knife hand technique performed in kata.

LUNG #5 (L-5)

L-5 is located approximately 2 AU or 1 inch in from the outside edge of the elbow crease, and 1 AU or 1/2 inch down on the inside of the forearm. Striking this point down and towards the hand causes the knees to buckle and creates multiple creases/ folds in the body.

For me, L-5 has become one of the most used pressure points. Its use is essential for helping create imbalance in the body's structure. Being located on

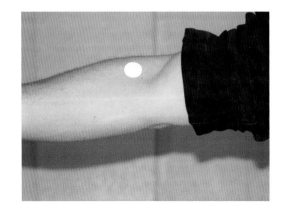

the arm, allows for easy access and manipulation, especially in grab situations. In the following sequence, LU #5 is initially used to destroy the structure of the attacker's body to set up a throwing technique.

In Figure 290, the defender strikes L-5 on the attacker's grabbing arm, creasing the body and buckling the knees. This motion brings the head forward for a hair grab that torques the spine and arches the attacker (Figure 291).

In Figure 292, the defender rotates, twisting and locking the spinal structure, while keeping the attacker's elbow tight to the body. This arches the spine and brings the attacker's head out beyond his base (feet).

In Figure 293, the defender removes his left leg (attacker's triangle balance point), stepping behind and throwing attacker to the ground.

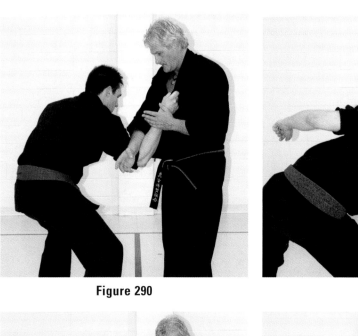

Figure 290   **Figure 291**

Figure 292   **Figure 293**

Basic Pressure Points of The Head and Neck

In this section we locate, and explain some points on the head and neck, that are easily accessible for use in hand combination striking, or attacking with finger pressure in a grab situation.

Remember that attacking pressure point meridians on the arms will activate these head/neck points, making them more sensitive and effective.

STOMACH #9 (S-9)

This point is located in the inside crease of the sternocleidomastoid muscle of the neck, level with the Adam's apple. The angle and direction for attacking this point is a 45-degree angle into the neck.

One self-defense application for attacking S-9 would involve slipping inside the attacker's right punch while striking the attacking arm with a right knife hand to L-6 (Figure 294).

Immediately following the strike to the attacker's arm, the defender strikes into the crease of the sternocleidomastoid muscle, into the neck (Figure 295).

This point may also be struck with a spear hand thrust, seen in many traditional kata (Figure 296).

| **Figure 294** | **Figure 295** | **Figure 296** |

STOMACH #5 (S-5)

ST-5 is the intersecting point of the two branches of the Stomach meridian, on the face and head. This point lies under the jaw, about one third of the way from the corner of the jaw, in the indentation. This point is to be struck upward towards the center of the head.

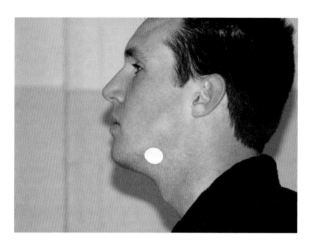

This point may be struck using several different, attacking weapons. In Figure 297, the defender is using an elbow to strike the arched opponent. Note the position of the head, with the chin manipulated upward.

In Figure 298, the defender uses a palm strike to attack ST-5, on a manipulated attacker. The spear hand thrust is also an applicable weapon to attack this point.

Figure 297

Figure 298

TRIPLE WARMER #17 (TW-17)

TW-17 is located under the ear, in the crease behind the jaw. Obviously, due to the location, this point needs to be struck back to front.

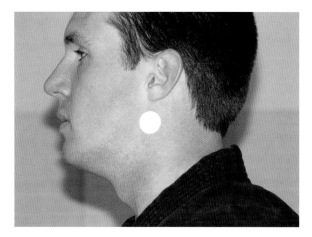

This point may be struck on an opponent whose structure has been manipulated to expose this area of the jaw. This may be done by creasing the folds of the body through striking or manipulation. (Figure 299)

Figure 299

LARGE INTESTINE #18

LI-18 is located directly under the ear, level with the Adam's apple. The point is located on the outside edge of the sternocleidomastoid muscle. Strike this point towards the center of the neck.

In Figure 300, the attacker throws a right punch, the defender slips out to angle #3 and executes a parry block. After parrying the strike, the defender extends the right arm slightly. This pre-positions the right hand, to strike LI-18 on the attacker's secondary rotation.

As the attacker rotates to throw the left punch, the defender strikes LI-18 with a right ridge hand. This strike is accompanied by a left palm strike to TW-23. (Figure 301)

Figure 300

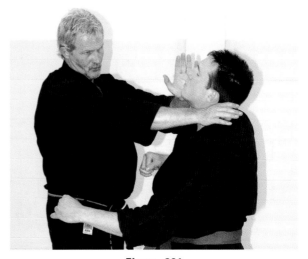

Figure 301

TRIPLE WARMER #23 (TW-23)

TW-23 is located in the depression of the temple, near the edge of the eyebrow. *WARNING: This point is never to be struck while training! Severe damage can result from hitting this point!*

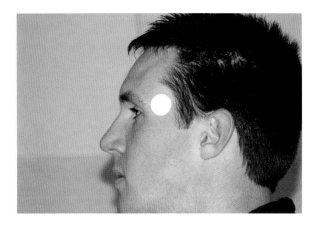

TW-23 can also be attacked using the hammer fist, as in the Naihanchi kata. In Figure 302, the defender slips out to angle #3 and parries the incoming punch.

As the defender starts his rotation to throw the left punch, the defender strikes with a hammer fist to TW-23. (Figure 303)

| **Figure 302** | **Figure 303** |

In this chapter, we focused on some basic pressure points that are applicable in many self-defense situations. These are by no means the only points a practitioner should study. This information is merely a guide to get you started on using pressure points in your practice.

Familiarize yourself with these points, and how they lie in between the muscle groups or crevices of the body. When experimenting with these points, notice how they affect the balance and structure, of your opponent. Also experiment with your escaping/ repositioning arts, as well as your manipulation of the attacker's structure, to set up the body for striking these points.

CHAPTER 14

Conclusion

The journey of a martial artist is not an easy one. A good martial artist has a code in which he or she does the best they can to live by. Attempting to live by a code of honor, respect, compassion, and constant growth and improvement, is not an easy path. But, it is a rewarding one! Especially for the practitioner, who chooses to become a teacher of the martial arts.

We all know of students who are lured to the martial arts by its mystique. They set out with visions of attaining a state of total self-confidence. When the newness of their training wears off, and they come to realize that this process, or path, requires constant struggle to achieve growth, their interest and excitement begins to fade. Constant repetition of technique, constant correction by the sensei, and the constant struggle to become a better martial artist and person, can be a really scary thing for many people.

As martial artists, we deal with physical conflict in our training on a daily basis. The physical conflict in the dojo is a microcosm of life. Everyday, in no matter what walk of life, no matter what our personal or professional activities may be, we all deal with some sort of conflict. We all have a certain amount of conflict inside us. The battle is the same as that of the one within the dojo.

As with the constant struggle for improvement in the arts, the writing of this book has been a similar struggle. Words are an extremely difficult means of communication, especially when written. But because of that challenge or struggle, there has been a great amount of growth for myself, and my students.

The incredible impact of the lessons and philosophies of my teachers have, without a doubt, helped me through some of the toughest periods of my life. In this book, I have tried to challenge the readers to look deeper into their martial art, and explore the concepts and how they can relate and enhance what they already do. This text is meant to act as a guideline, giving direction for exploration and experimentation. Remember that it is important to refer back to this information, for every time you do, your understanding should intensify and expand.

Since this text is as much about philosophy and dealing with conflicts that exist in everyone's life, I again challenge you, the reader, to internalize and start to apply these philosophies in your everyday life. It is my hope that some of what is written here may help you in your study of the martial arts, and your study of balance in everyday life.

Jeff Driscoll, Sensei

Acknowledgements

I would like to take this opportunity to thank all the people who have contributed to my development. Without their direction and advice this book would never have be written. First of all, I would like to thank the instructors who've made an impact on my martial arts and my life.

There are two people who, other than my parents, have been the most influential in my life. They would be Hanshi Bruce Juchnik, my Kosho Ryu Kempo teacher; and Shihan Carl Long, my Eishin Ryu Iaijutsu teacher. I'd like to thank them for all the guidance and support they've given me through the years. They both have shown me a different way of looking at things.

Under their instruction, I have learned martial arts concepts and philosophies that have truly changed my life for the better. It is said that a good teacher can take you places you've never been, but a great teacher can significantly change the place you're in. I am forever in their debt for dramatically changing my life for the better.

Next I would like to thank Masayuki Shimabukuro Hanshi, who I met through Shihan Long. Shimabukuro Hanshi, the author of *Flashing Steel*, has, through his writings and personal contact, opened doors for me in my swordsmanship and in the way I look at life.

I would also like to thank Kyoshi Pat Kelly and Kyoshi Larry Kraxberger for their guidance and their patience. They both have contributed so much to my growth as a martial artist and as a person.

I would also like to thank Shihan Tony Annesi, for introducing me to conceptual martial arts and Master George Dillman for his instruction in the area of pressure points and Kyusho Jutsu.

A special thanks also goes out to all of my students who contributed to the completion of this text: Tom Smith, John Kelly, Rick Alexander, Wes Schwartz, John Pothering, Ed Miller, Brian Cooper, Linda Mullins, and Angie and Drew Knott.

Special thanks goes out to Cindy Jutras for her work in editing this text as well as her calligraphy, and to Jon Ludwig Shihan for the layout and design of the original work. Thanks to Alexzander Warasta for his pictures of the Shaka-In Temple. Instructional photos were taken by Linda Mullins. Japan photos were taken by Jeff Driscoll.

And last but certainly not least, I want to thank Jennifer Jordan. It is due to her inspiration and belief in me that this book was compiled and completed.

About the Author

Jeff Driscoll Shihan

Jeff Driscoll has been a student of the martial arts for 28 years. He has been the owner and instructor at the Driscoll Institute of the Martial Arts in Pottsville, PA, since 1986.

Driscoll Sensei holds ranks of 5th Dan in Ryu Kyu Kempo Karate, 4th Dan in Kosho Ryu Kempo, 3rd Dan in Muso Jikden Eishin Ryu Iaijutsu, and a 1st Dan in Tae Kwon Do. He currently studies and teaches Kosho Ryu Kempo, as a student of Hanshi Bruce Juchnik, and Muso Jikiden Eishin Ryu Iaijutsu, under Shihan Carl Long and Hanshi Masayuki Shimabukuro .

Driscoll Sensei has also been the host of the East Coast Gathering since 1998, an event geared towards bringing martial artists together from different styles and systems, in an atmosphere of sharing and learning.

Contact Information:
Driscoll Institute of Martial Arts21 N. Centre Pottsville, PA 17901.
Email: senseijd2000@yahoo.com
www.driscollinstitute.com

Come visit our store at www.zanshinproducts.net

Memories

Oregon Summer Retreat 1986

Terry Webb, Michael Brown, Bruce Juchnik,
Jeff Driscoll, Larry Kraxberger, Marc Burnham

The First East Coast Gathering 1998

Larry Kraxberger, Pat Kelly, Jeff Driscoll, Bruce Juchnik,
Michael Brown, Terry Webb, Marc Burnham (bottom)

The Gathering San Diego 2000

Professor Wally Jay, Jeff Driscoll, Pat Kelly

The Gathering Reno 2007

Hanshi Paul Yamaguchi, Jeff Driscoll

Japan Trip 2005

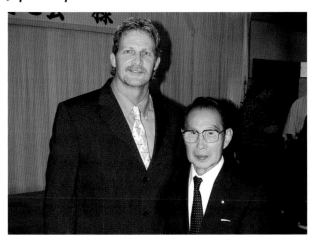

Jeff Driscoll, Miura Hanshi

Dillman International Event 1992

Ron Richards, Sandra Schlessman, Jeff Driscoll

Eishin Ryu Iaijutsu Instructors 2007

Carl Long, Jeff Driscoll, Shimabukuru Sensei

Japan Trip 2005

Jeff Driscoll and Rick Alexander at Yagyu Village

Japan Trip 2005

Jeff Driscoll, Shimabukuru Sensei,
and Carl Long at Yagyu Village

Japan Trip 2005

Jeff Driscoll, Carl Long, Rick Alexander